A View
from the
Buggy

Jerry S. Eicher
Nathan Miller

HARVEST HOUSE PUBLISHERS
EUGENE, OREGON

Unless otherwise indicated, all Scripture quotations are from the King James Version of the Bible.

Cover by Garborg Design Works, Savage, Minnesota

Cover photos © Chris Garborg; hendrsd / Bigstock

A VIEW FROM THE BUGGY

Copyright © 2014 by Jerry S. Eicher and Nathan Miller
Published by Harvest House Publishers
Eugene, Oregon 97402
www.harvesthousepublishers.com

Library of Congress Cataloging-in-Publication Data
Eicher, Jerry S.
A view from the buggy / Jerry S. Eicher and Nathan Miller.
    pages cm
ISBN 978-0-7369-5686-4 (pbk.)
ISBN 978-0-7369-5687-1 (eBook)
1. Christian life—Amish authors. 2. Simplicity—Religious aspects—Christianity. I. Title.
BX8129.A5E33 2014
289.7'3—dc23

                                                                    2013043550

Printed in the United States of America

14 15 16 17 18 19 20 21 22 / VP-JH / 10 9 8 7 6 5 4 3 2 1

Contents

A Horse Named Rose

Jerry Eicher

*Give to him that asketh thee, and from him that would
borrow of thee turn not thou away (Matthew 5:42).*

HUMILITY IS VALUED BY THE AMISH COMMUNITY, RIGHT UP THERE
after godliness. Every member is expected to readily admit to his or
her shortcomings. So I will open this book of true Amish stories with
a tale from my family's repertoire of less-than-stellar accomplishments.

County Road 96 runs through the center of the little Amish community in Belle Center, Ohio, where our family had moved upon our
return from several years in Honduras. Our time in Honduras had
been a mixture of good and bad, but our return home was disappoint-
ing to the whole family.

Dad had come up to the states some months earlier and made the
down payment on the property that would be our new home. When
he returned, he made a point of telling us that our neighbors, Eldon
Yoder and his wife, Fannie, were friendly folks, as were other folks in
the Amish community.

I was 16 at the time and mourned our move away from Honduras.
This preempted any interest I had in who our new neighbors would be.
But when we arrived in Belle Center, Dad was proved right—the Yod-
ers were fine, generous people. This was made clear when, upon our
arrival, Eldon Yoder offered to sell us Rose, his best horse.

Eldon Yoder was a short man with a bushy beard. His wife, Fannie,
was always smiling. She was almost as tall as her husband, and a fluttering sort of woman. Fannie gave off a sense of eternal busyness, which
contrasted with the easygoing nature of her husband.

If Eldon had any regrets about the sale of Rose, I never heard him say so. And one would have heard such a thing in that small community. I hasten to add that Rose was a gentle, mild-natured horse when we bought her. This was one of her attractive qualities, Dad claimed. We didn't need a dashing horse. We had arrived back Stateside bruised in heart and soul. A troublesome horse was the last thing we needed. Maybe that knowledge was what had stirred Eldon Yoder's compassion to sell Rose to us—or perhaps it was simply our general bedraggled condition.

Sadly, the sale of Rose to our family—though well-intentioned—quickly turned into a disaster. What happened, we never really knew. But something went wrong as we proceeded that turned a kind gesture sour. Not intentionally, of course. It just sort of happened. Dad knew how to handle horses, and he didn't abuse them. He had been around horses all of his life.

I know we liked the calm and gentle Rose and expected that she'd be a fine horse for us. But to our surprise—and no doubt Eldon Yoder's too—she was soon ruined beyond repair. Perhaps she didn't like this Amish family who had spent time in faraway Honduras. Whatever the reason, Rose began to balk. When hitched to a buggy, she simply refused to go.

This is not only a most inconvenient trait for an Amish horse to have, but a well-nigh intolerable one. The whole family would cram into the buggy outside whatever farm the church service had been held at that Sunday. People were milling around, talking with each other as the Amish do after the services—and there we were, right in the middle of the driveway, with Rose refusing to budge.

Dad would slap the reins and holler for Rose to go. Nothing happened! Rose stayed stubbornly in place. She'd even rear a little off her front feet, but she made no other movement. Next, we'd climb out of the buggy and pull on her bridle. This only angered Rose, causing her to rear higher and paw the air. We were the embarrassment of the Sunday afternoon church gathering.

Eldon Yoder would come by and talk to Rose. He'd speak in soft, soothing words of comfort. But his touch no longer did any good. Rose didn't plan to move for the Eichers until she was good and ready, and that was often a longer time than we cared to wait. The funny thing was that once Rose *did* take off, she hightailed it out of the lane so fast Dad could barely hang on to the lines.

This was a situation that couldn't continue for long. Dad tried every method of curing Rose he could think of. Every Amish horseman's trick in the book, Dad tried. Nothing worked.

A horse that won't cooperate isn't much good to an Amish man. So, sad to say, in the end, the inevitable happened. Dad had to sell Rose to the buyer of last resort: the local butcher shop. No one else wanted a balking horse.

It troubled us greatly—this gentle horse we had somehow ruined. We questioned the integrity of our souls. Weren't horses a decent judge of one's character? Had we failed as a family to make Rose feel at home with us? No matter how hard we tried to figure out what had gone wrong, we came to a dead end every time.

Through it all Eldon Yoder and his wife, Fannie, were our greatest comforters. They assured us that this could have happened to anyone. Not one incriminating word was ever spoken by them against this new family who had come from the ends of the earth to settle in the community.

I'm not sure I could have done the same if Eldon Yoder and his family had ruined my best horse. Eldon was a good man who knew how to give away what God had placed in his hands and to fully let it go. I wish I could always say the same of myself.

Color Tour

Nathan Miller

*And let the beauty of the LORD our God be upon us: and
establish thou the work of our hands upon us; yea, the
work of our hands establish thou it (Psalm 90:17).*

COME HERE, THUNDER! COME HERE!" I CALLED AS I CROSSED OUR
pasture. Thunder was our faithful standardbred buggy horse. I had
equipped myself with a scoop of his favorite feed and a lead rope.
I approached cautiously, knowing that pushing him usually didn't
work. Thunder was a suspicious horse and easily turned tail. Thankfully, today Thunder cooperated and I snapped the lead rope to his
halter. We headed for the barn.

The autumn day was comfortable, neither too hot nor too cold. The
sky was clear and the family's excitement high. My wife, Mattie, and
I had made plans for a fall color tour with our three daughters and a
friend named Delores. Taking time out for a family ride along with a
picnic lunch would be a special treat for all of us.

"Okay, are we ready?" I asked after I hitched Thunder to the buggy.

"Yes! Yes!" came the happy chorus.

"Giddap, Thunder," I said, and we were on our way. Thunder wasn't
in a hurry and neither were we. The picture-perfect day matched our
spirits as we slowly *clip-clopped* our way to deacon Omer Schrock's
house to pick up Delores. Here we exchanged our buggy for their one-
horse wagon, which provided more room and a better view of the
scenery.

The late September countryside in rural Michigan was beautiful. We were headed eight miles to the northwest where the elevation
climbed, allowing us to look out over the valley in which our small
Amish community was settled.

We relaxed and chatted as our wagon wheels slowly ate away the miles. The pace afforded plenty of time to visit, notice the birds singing, rabbits hopping, and squirrels scampering.

We crossed the Muskegon River and turned left on River Road. The trees were stunning along this back route, bursting with varied hues of bright reds, yellows, and gaudy oranges. The traffic was low and the *English* people were friendly. Most of them waved as they passed our wagon.

We must have been a rare treat for one man. He quickly pulled out his camera and took our picture as we approached. He barely had time to jump out of the way of an oncoming car as we passed each other. We waved to him and he waved back. We chuckled as we continued our journey.

"At least we made his day," I remarked to Mattie. "Apparently he doesn't see too many horses travel this road."

I soon pointed to my right. "Look at this, girls!" Someone had carved an impressive totem pole using a variety of animals. An eagle topped the pole. This was the first totem pole our children had seen in real life. We probably would have missed the delight if we had hurried by in a faster vehicle.

As we approached our destination, the road steepened and I had to urge Thunder to keep on the move. This was a longer drive than he usually took. But we soon turned onto the final stretch, a small dirt road not much wider than a two-track. We climbed the last half mile and we were there.

The view so far had been pretty, but here, looking out over the valley with the forests in crimson colors broken by the fields, it was awesome. Farms dotted the hillside here and there. Cars meandered down the ribbon roads, appearing small from our vantage point. All was peaceful and quiet as we sat on a log munching fresh popcorn and drinking lemonade. Thunder was tied close by, gratefully resting up for his return trip.

For a moment our little group sat quietly absorbing the tranquility and beauty. We were amazed how far we could see across the valley. We could even recognize a building that belonged to one of the Amish homes.

"It looks much farther than it actually is," I remarked.

"That's right, it does," Mattie agreed. "This is so special. We get to spend time together and enjoy God's handiwork."

"I really enjoy this," I said in approval.

About then Delores had a suggestion. "Let's go for a walk. There's a trail that runs through the woods over there." She pointed to a beautiful stand of hardwoods on the right.

"Yes, let's," the children consented happily.

We slowly rose from our special log seat and stretched. We gathered the remaining picnic supplies and loaded them on the wagon for when we would later leave. Thunder was happily munching the tender grass, enjoying his break. We meandered slowly down the trail, fully enjoying this time of togetherness and family happiness.

How blessed we are, I meditated. *Thank You, Father, for giving me a beautiful, loving family. I have much more than I deserve. Thank You for Your love and care.*

Eventually I announced with reluctance, "I believe it's time to get back and head for home."

"Oh, please, just a little longer," the children begged.

"I'm sorry, but we must get home before it's too late," I said. "Perhaps we can come again next fall."

"Yes, let's," they agreed.

"Maybe we should make this a yearly tradition," Mattie suggested.

"I think that would be a great idea," I agreed.

Minutes later, the family had climbed aboard the wagon for home.

"Is everyone loaded and ready?" I asked before I untied Thunder. When there was a chorus of "Yes," I turned the wagon around, climbed aboard, and we began to retrace the eight miles back home.

"That was really worthwhile," I told Mattie. "Thank you for suggesting it."

"Oh, you're welcome," Mattie said with a smile. "It was really special."

Everyone was quiet and seemed a bit tired on the trip back. Emilee, the youngest, snuggled on my lap and was soon fast asleep. We traveled in comfortable silence, each lost in his or her own thoughts.

Thunder eagerly pulled the wagon along. He sensed we were headed home and had an extra spring to his steps. In no time we crossed the river and reached the Schrock residence.

We thanked Delores, glad that she had accompanied us, and hitched Thunder to our own buggy. We loaded one last time and *clip-clopped* the last stretch home. After we unhitched Thunder we unloaded the buggy. Thunder was turned out to pasture tired and happy, as we headed for the house feeling no less so.

Going Fishing

Erma Louise Schrock

*And he shall turn the heart of the fathers to the children,
and the heart of the children to their fathers, lest I come
and smite the earth with a curse (Malachi 4:6).*

ONE BRIGHT DAY IN JUNE OUR FAMILY WAS SITTING AT THE LUNCH
table. Rapid conversation was flowing as everyone shared their bit of
news from the day's happenings so far.

My brother Alvin piped up, "Dad! I talked with Jesse this morning. He's wondering if we fellows want to go fishing this evening. He'll
pick us up in his van."

Our brother Aaron wasted no time in answering that question. "Yes,
let's."

Dad took a little more time to think this through. He glanced
toward Mom. "Is there something else planned for this evening?"

"Not that I know of," Mom said. "Other than a quiet night at home."

"Please...let's go," the boys begged Dad.

Dad finally nodded. "I'm in favor, and I think I'll go along."

"What about me?" I asked. "I'm the oldest girl. Do I get to go even
if Jesse didn't mention me?"

Jesse was our next door neighbor and an older man. He was a retired
school teacher and spoke with a British accent. He sounded really intelligent. We children would hang around and enjoy his stories when he
stopped by for a visit.

"Do you want to?" Dad had a smile on his face, but he already knew
that answer. If Jesse was taking the boys finishing, I certainly wanted
to go along.

"I'm sure Jesse wouldn't mind you tagging along," Nelson spoke up.

I wasn't convinced and looked skeptically at Mom. She shrugged. "Whatever Dad thinks is fine with me."

"Then may I?" I was getting excited now.

Dad's smile grew broader. "Yes, I think you can." And so it was decided.

Alvin had to warn me, though. "Be ready exactly at six."

"I can handle that," I said. I was already looking forward to getting out of the house for a while. What a great treat!

The rest of the afternoon seemed to drag until it had slowed down to a snail's pace. Finally, six o'clock rolled around. As Mom and I washed the last of the dinner dishes, a small blue minivan glided into the driveway.

"Jesse's here!" I shouted, and looked hopefully at Mom. "May I go now?"

"Of course," Mom said. "I'll finish up with your sisters."

"Thanks," I whispered, and slipped into my flip-flops.

"Enjoy yourself," Mom said as I went out the door.

"Don't worry, I will," I hollered over my shoulder.

I approached the van, and a sudden shyness swept over me. I quietly joined Dad and Alvin, who were packing the last of the fishing devices.

Jesse peered out of the van. "Well…hello! So you're going along?"

"Hi." I tried to smile. "I guess so."

Jesse didn't seem to object and my pounding heart slowed down.

Dad shoved the cooler into the back of the van and said, "I think we're all set now. Everyone hop in."

"Where will I sit?" I whispered to Alvin.

"You can sit in the backseat with me," Alvin suggested, so I wiggled in beside him while the rest found their seats around us.

We're actually going, I thought with excitement.

I leaned toward Alvin. "How long does it take to get there?"

"About fifteen minutes," Alvin explained as the van rolled out of the lane.

I settled back and watched the landscape pass by with one ear open to the guys' conversation.

"Why aren't we driving to the lake in our buggy?" I interrupted to ask Alvin.

"We could have," Alvin said, "but it's better this way. The lake only allows access to the property owners living around it or to the people they know. We'd cause too many questions driving in with our buggy."

That made sense, and I went back to looking out of the van windows.

"I think we're getting close," Alvin finally said. He pointed to a large welcome sign marking the entrance to Lake Miramichi. We followed the winding lane and parked close to the water's edge. Someone pushed open the van doors and out we tumbled.

"Come with me," Dad said as he picked up the tackle box, fishing pole, and a bucket.

I pulled my rod out of the back of the van. "Do we have worms?" I asked.

Nelson handed me a Folger's coffee can full of wiggling night crawlers. "Here are some for you."

I took the can with one hand and followed Dad as he led the way to the beach area, where we found a pretty spot along the bank. The rest of the group also settled in. I gazed around in wonder at the beauty of the place.

Dad interrupted my pleasant thoughts when he handed me a worm. "Tear this long one apart so we don't waste anything."

I wrinkled my nose as I tried to get a grip on the slimy thing. I clutched the worm with both hands and gave a mighty jerk. The deed was done. Dad took one end and I was left with the other piece.

"Can you bait your own hook?" Dad asked.

"The boys showed me how at home," I said, but I held my breath as I slid the worm on the hook. Afterward I bent over to rinse my hand in the lake water and rose to my feet again. I gave the line a fling and ever so slowly reeled the line in. Dad gave his rod another toss, which sent his line way beyond where mine had landed.

"How do you cast it out so far?" I asked.

Dad jiggled his line. "You give the rod a good, firm cast and release the button just as you finish your swing."

"I wish you'd watch and see if I do it right," I said.

"Just a minute." Dad finished reeling his line in. "Okay. Go for it."

I took a good grip and gave my best cast. It fell short of where I wanted it, but Dad didn't appear discouraged. "Practice, practice, practice," he said.

I smiled and reeled in slowly. The line bobbed.

"Set your hook!" Dad hollered.

I hauled back and wailed when the now empty line flew out over the water. Dad only smiled. "Practice, practice, practice."

I cast my line again, and there it was. Another bite. I set my hook and squealed, "I got him!"

"Bring it in," Dad encouraged. "Keep reeling."

The next moment I had a good-sized fish out of the water.

"That's a nice bluegill." Dad beamed. "Can you unhook it?"

"No," I said. Dread filled my mind. Surely Dad wouldn't make me learn how to unhook a fish this evening. But my fears soon came true.

Dad calmly stepped closer. "I'll show you how, and the next time you can do it." He pointed. "Here are the gills, so slip your hand down like this." He demonstrated, grasping the fish. "Push the hook down like this, and there you go." Dad finished and threw the fish into the bucket.

How will I ever get a grip like that on a slippery fish? I wondered with wide eyes.

Dad had already gone back to fishing, so I cast once more. In no time I had another fish.

"I still can't do it," I moaned to Dad.

"It's part of the fun," Dad said. "It's not as hard as it looks."

I took a deep breath and slipped my left hand over the fish's face. Dad smiled as I seized the hook. Slowly I pushed down, and amazingly I had it unhooked.

"Good job," Dad cheered.

I felt warm all over. "You're right," I told him. "It works if you just do it."

We were soon back to fishing, the rest of the evening passing swiftly. We released the smaller fish but kept the larger ones.

Just before sunset Dad announced, "I think we should gather up our things and head home."

"Already?" I groaned. "I'm enjoying myself."

"It's after nine." Alvin seconded Dad's opinion, and I knew we'd have to leave. Moments later we loaded everything into the van, and I settled into the backseat again.

"I hope we can do this again," I whispered to Alvin.

"So do I," Alvin agreed.

I figured I'd smile a long time over this wonderful evening. And to think that God had made such amazing things as fish. He must be a very great God.

Horses and Boys

Marvin Wengerd

Can two walk together, except they be agreed? (Amos 3:3)

WHEN I WAS A BOY WE LIVED ON A SMALL FARM IN WALNUT CREEK VAL-
ley. Back then farms with waving fields of grain and sprawling cornfields stretched their yellow and green across the valley. The "big creek,"
as we boys called Walnut Creek, tumbled its course to the river that lay
beyond. This creek marked the southern boundary of our farm.

Up from the big creek toward the house was a 12-acre bottom field
in which we grew corn. In the spring came plowing, disking, and har-
rowing. Planting followed. Then cultivation. Row after row, hour after
hour of sitting on a two-horse cultivator swatting flies, steering the
lines, and managing fast foot pedal plunges to miss hitting tender corn
seedlings.

This all led toward monotony, of course. King and Queen, our half
wild, half tame team, needed to rest at times, so the monotony was broken by end-of-row breaks where reading and tossing stones in the creek
were favorite pastimes while we waited.

When the corn was waist high, cultivating was over and summer
with all its work and play began. Making hay, shocking, and then
threshing wheat and oats and chasing groundhogs and each other
made the sweat run down our backs. It also added inches to our biceps
as summer moved into fall. By then the memories of our hard days cultivating were all but forgotten. The trees had begun to color and the
cornfields had turned from a sea of green to a rustling golden brown.
Harvest time had arrived.

The cool October wind not only stole summer's warmth and fun, but it also reminded Dad that it was time to pick corn. Years before, Dad had invested in a two-row corn picker—my brother and me.

We would hitch King and Queen to our hay wagon equipped with one-foot-high sides all around. Off we jolted to the waiting cornfields. Our right hands were fitted with leather bands and sported V-shaped metal hooks on the palm side. With this outfit we tore into a corn husk and ripped it from the stalk. And with speed that's hard to explain, the left hand grabbed the well-guarded ear and yanked it free. With the same left hand the ear is airborne to find its place on the wagon bed with a dull thud. Over and over down the seemingly endless field my Dad's two-row picker ripped, grabbed, yanked, and threw corn.

As we picked (such a simple word for a very difficult job!) corn, the wagon with King and Queen hitched to it moved along as well. We would start at the back of the wagon and work our way up to the front, filling as we went.

Standing at the front of the wagon we would simply holler, "Giddap" to King and Queen. They would start off; the two most recently picked corn rows guiding them in a straight line.

When we were ready for them to stop we'd call out, "Whoa!" The wagon would have moved ten feet or so by then, and obediently the horses would stop, even though the lines hung limply on the wagon. Horsemen call this *voice command*.

"Whoa." "Giddap." "Whoa." "Giddap." "Whoa." "Giddap." All morning long King and Queen started and stopped perfectly as my brother and I fought cold hands and picked corn.

We had just unloaded and were back out on the west end of the field, farthest away from the barn, when the incident occurred. The wagon being empty, the corn landed on the wooden wagon floor with a sharp crack, kernels flying in all directions.

"Giddap," I called and kept on picking corn, throwing it into the empty wagon. "Whoa," I shouted above the rustling corn. "That's far enough."

But somehow wild King didn't hear my command. Both horses kept going, spooked by the sound of the corn. Jumping out of my corn row with my heart pounding in my throat, I yelled with all the force of my 12-year-old vocal chords. "Whoa! Whoa! Whoa!"

Nothing slowed them down. In fact, they picked up speed.

Tears pushed their way into my eyes as I thought of what could happen when King and Queen reached a gallop. They were headed straight for the road and the barn beyond. Visions of them meeting the milk truck barreling down the road flashed before me. And how would the barn door look after these two had tried to funnel themselves through its narrow opening?

But when the team was only a few yards from the road, I saw that King and Queen were galloping headlong into another kind of problem. My breath was lost and my heart raced as I watched in disbelief as the two horses made straight for an electric pole. Wild-eyed King, every muscle straining, pulled to the right as he tried to avoid the pole. He might have succeeded but for Queen's 1,800 pounds that pulled in the other direction, also to avoid the pole. Straining with all her might, Queen held her course. The thundering noise seemed to put wings to the team's feet as the two hit the pole with the wagon tongue in the middle, flying like an arrow from the bow.

The almost empty wagon careened wildly sideways across the corn rows, crashing nearby stalks to the ground. Harnesses strained as the heads of the two horses met on the far side of the pole in a face-to-face encounter. With heaving breath, they pulled their heads apart.

My brother and I approached with knees shaking. Would there be pieces of their harness and wagon tongue left to pick up?

Amazingly nothing was much amiss, other than King and Queen regarding each other in puzzled wonderment.

Unable to contain our pent-up emotions, we burst out laughing. What had started as a world-sized catastrophe ended with two boys holding their sides over two horses with 12 acres and a road to run away in, but who had been stopped because they couldn't agree which side of the pole to go around.

An Eventful Evening

Janice Hochstetler

*What is man, that thou art mindful of him? and the
son of man, that thou visitest him? (Psalm 8:4)*

IT WAS HUMID THAT SUNDAY, AND EVERYONE FELT HOT AND A BIT
grumpy as we drove home from the three-hour church service. Our
horse, Lady, plodded along, her hooves beating rhythmically on the
pavement. Moments later, Mom turned around in the front seat of the
buggy to ask, "Why don't we go down to the pond for a picnic supper?"

There was a chorus of, "Yes, let's," from the rest of the children, and
I joined in with enthusiasm.

"May we go swimming?" nine-year-old Jeffery asked from his perch
between his brother and sister on the back seat of the surrey.

"Not today," Dad said. "It's Sunday."

Jeffery groaned. "It won't be any fun if we can't swim."

Dad kept his voice firm. "You can go wading, but no swimming."

Jeffery accepted the verdict with a sigh, and there were no more
protests. We soon arrived home and were on the way down the dusty
cow path behind the barn. Down the lane that led to the woods where,
inside the leafy shadows, lay the pond.

I watched as Dad started a fire when we arrived. He planned to grill
the hamburgers Mom had brought along. They would be scrumptious,
since they came from our own Angus beef, raised on the farm.

While the fire died down, Dad and the boys decided to move the
paddleboat we kept at the pond. As they lifted the boat near the shore,
a skunk scurried away toward the field nearby.

"Eeeek!" I squealed and jumped back a few feet.

Six-year-old Jaylin held his nose. "I'm glad she didn't spray me."

The smell was bad enough already. What would it be like to have skunk spray all over oneself? There would have been little choice then but to dive into the pond, even with Dad's prohibition on Sunday swimming.

I shivered as the skunk disappeared from sight. Jeffery, though, had already forgotten his scare and was headed off into the tall grass. Moments later, his loud yell sent another chill up my back. I turned to see what trouble had appeared now. But instead of trouble, a beautiful fawn leaped over the grass. My heart beat faster at the wonderful sight. God has made such graceful creatures, and so fragile. He is a great and wonderful God indeed.

By the time the fawn disappeared, Dad had returned to his fire and the hamburgers were put on. When they were finally cooked, we ate near the water's edge to the sound of chirping birds and croaking frogs.

After supper Dad asked, "Who wants a paddleboat ride?"

"Me!" Jeffery shouted much louder than necessary.

"Me too!" Jaylin was jumping up and down in excitement. Two-year-old Justin, who had no fear of water, echoed the words.

I didn't want to miss out on the fun, so I added my desire. But before we could leave Mom said, "Why don't we all help clean up the supper mess, then we can go together for a ride?"

We all agreed, even the smaller children, and finished in no time.

The boat was large enough to hold us all, and we piled in. As we headed across the water, the sounds of nature surrounded us. It was a gorgeous and peaceful evening now that the sun was down.

We had passed the middle of the pond, which Dad had once claimed was 15 feet deep, and were approaching the opposite shoreline when Jeffery cried out, "Dad, the boat is going down. Water's about to come in."

"We need to go for the shore!" Dad's usually calm voice was frantic.

Then, without further warning, the water began pouring in. Dad panicked and jumped to his feet. For a moment he stood there frozen, when *splash*, the back of the boat was under the water and we tipped sideways. This dumped all of us into the cool water. Most of us screamed for help and thought we would drown, since Dad and Jeffery were the only ones who could swim. The lifejackets were still on the boat.

I sank under the water, where I grasped for something to hold on to. My hand caught ahold of Mom's dress, and I clung to it with all my might. I remember thinking that I had read somewhere that this was something one should never do, as the other person would only be dragged under as well. So I let go, but kicked wildly and thrashed about.

"Jesus, please help me," I prayed, although I'm sure no one heard me but God Himself. My head bobbed to the surface and I gasped for air. I saw the boat floating upside down, with several of the family clinging to it. I grabbed and hung on myself.

"Okay, everyone hang on," Dad hollered. "I will pull the boat and swim for shore."

Jeffery had already taken off for shore. We could see him swim his hardest. Jaylin and Justin were screaming hysterically. Thankfully Mom had been holding Justin's hand when we tipped, and she still had ahold of him when she came up. Mom tried to comfort him, but to no avail.

By now Jeffery had reached the shore and looked back, not sure how to help his terrified family.

Moments later Dad called out, "I can touch the bottom."

We still hung on as Dad pulled and pushed the boat closer to shore. When we finally emerged dripping wet, Dad sent up his own prayer, "Thank You, Lord!"

"What happened?" I asked as I wrung out my dress the best I could.

"We must have had too much weight for the boat," Dad winced. "Water must have seeped up between the compartments. But thankfully the boat kept afloat after we tipped. I never could have gotten you out any other way."

It was a sobering thought. We could all have drowned. We kept up our whispered thanks to God, and I added my own, "Thank You, Jesus, for helping us. Thank You that I still have both of my parents and all of my brothers."

Since we were all soaked now, there was nothing to do but gather up our supper items and head back up the cow path.

"Well, I guess you got your wish to go swimming," Dad cracked.

"But I didn't enjoy it one bit," Jeffery replied. He shivered even though he couldn't have been cold.

"And I didn't even lose my glasses," Mom added as another note of thanks.

And neither did I, I thought, as we walked toward home with very grateful hearts.

A Priceless Gift

Joanna Yoder

*As thou knowest not what is the way of the spirit, nor how the
bones do grow in the womb of her that is with child: even so thou
knowest not the works of God who maketh all (Ecclesiastes 11:5).*

WE WERE EXUBERANT. MOM HAD SAID THE BABY WOULD BE BORN THAT
night. We had been waiting for months. Now finally the time was
almost at hand when we would see our next sibling.

Mom and Dad had planned a home birth, so my four sisters and
I were sent downstairs to sleep in our basement bedrooms. But that
night, we girls chose to all crowd into one room together. Rebecca and
Anna Mary were in the bed, and Wilma, Rachel, and myself were on
a mattress on the floor.

Titus, our only brother and the oldest in the family, had gone to
his bedroom at the other end of the house. As the minutes ticked past,
four-year-old Rachel dropped off to sleep. But the rest of us were too
excited to sleep.

I knew the hour was late and we should get our rest, but thoughts
still raced through my mind. Thoughts like, *Will the baby be a boy or
a girl?*

I hoped for a boy. There were way too many girls already, and Titus
was 17. I figured he'd be excited to have a little brother. But whatever
God gave us, I knew we'd enjoy the baby. I was only 12, but I loved
babies.

My thoughts were interrupted when Rebecca flicked on a flashlight
and pointed it at the small clock perched on the shelf.

"What time is it?" I asked in a hushed voice.

"A little past twelve," she whispered. "Do you think the other girls
are sleeping?"

"I'm awake," Wilma piped up.

"Me too…", 11-year-old Anna Mary added.

"Well…let's all try to relax and sleep now," Rebecca said. At 15, she felt responsible for all of us.

"I'm too excited!" seven-year-old Wilma protested.

"We're all excited," Rebecca agreed. "But we need to sleep. Try counting backward from one thousand."

We all sighed and flopped back down on our pillows. Silence reigned again. I began counting backward and when I had reached 87, Rebecca sat straight up in bed. "I heard a baby cry!"

All thoughts of sleep fled as three more girls sat up, straining to hear any sound from upstairs.

It came soon enough. "Wa-a-ah!"

Now all four of us heard it plainly. We started laughing and hugging each other, twirling around the room. We bounced happily on the bed.

"We have a *baby*!" I squealed, forgetting that Rachel was still sleeping. But despite our noise, Rachel wasn't stirring.

"Do you think we could go upstairs?" I wondered aloud, hugging myself and bouncing some more.

"We'll wait until Dad comes down," Rebecca decided. "He promised to wake us once the baby arrived."

I knelt by the bedroom door and pressed my ear to the crack. Soon my sisters were beside me as we listened in the silence. We couldn't hear much, but with a little imagination we thought we heard a word or two. It sounded like Mom cooing, the way she did when she talked to a baby.

"Didn't she say *James Lee*?" I asked.

"It did almost sound like it," Rebecca agreed.

"It's a boy then!" Wilma declared.

We all knew James Lee was the name Mom and Dad had picked if the baby were a boy.

After what seemed like a long time there was a *thump, thump, thump* of feet on the stairs.

"That must be Dad!" Rebecca squealed.

We flung open the door and Dad appeared startled as four

nightgown-clad girls burst out, nearly bowling him over. I think he had expected to find us asleep.

"What is it?" one of us asked. "A boy or a girl?"

"It's a girl," Dad answered.

Disappointment filled my heart. How I had hoped for a little brother! But girls were just as sweet, I quickly told myself. The other girls had already stampeded up the stairs, and I turned to follow them. Eagerly we rounded the corner into the living room.

"Are you all still awake?" Mom greeted us in a surprised tone. Her eyes shone with joy and love. We knew she was glad we could see the baby so soon after she had been born.

But we were no longer looking at Mom. We crowded around Katie, the midwife, who had the baby wrapped snugly in a fuzzy blanket. We jostled each other in our attempt to get a good look at this new little family member. For a moment all was quiet as we gazed at the perfect little face.

"Oh…," I let out my breath, and everyone started to talk at once.

"She's so cute!"

"Look at all that hair!"

"Those tiny fingernails!"

"She looks like a china doll!"

"She's the cutest baby I've ever seen." That came from Titus, who had appeared behind us.

"Do you have a name picked out?" Katie asked.

"We'll call her Esther Marie," Dad said. He had a big grin on his face, and we knew he was as happy as the rest of us.

"I want to hold her," Anna Mary begged.

So, beginning with the oldest, we each had a turn at holding our tiny little sister. Titus got his turn too, and then Rebecca placed the baby in my arms.

I gazed at the oval-shaped face, the silky black hair, the tiny upturned nose. I exclaimed over the thin arms, the slender fingers, the narrow feet. Esther Marie squirmed in my arms and opened her eyes. This was followed by her mouth, and she stuck out her tiny pink tongue. My heart melted, and I didn't care one bit that she wasn't a boy. Girls were just as precious.

The baby was passed on to Anna Mary and last of all to Wilma. Then Mom reached for her, and Dad shooed us all back to bed.

"Go get some sleep," he ordered. "She'll still be here in the morning."

We filed downstairs and I nestled into the bed beside Rachel, who was still sound asleep. My heart overflowed with gratefulness to God.

"Thank You, Lord, for this priceless gift You have given us," I prayed. "Help me to always be a good example to her. Help her grow up to love and serve You." Moments later I drowsily drifted off to sleep.

The next morning, after I had eaten breakfast and admired Baby Esther some more, I declared to Rebecca, "I'm going to wake Rachel. It's almost nine and she doesn't even know we have a baby. She's slept long enough."

With those words I ran downstairs and entered the bedroom.

"Rachel, Rachel!" I called. "Wake up!"

She stirred, opened her large brown eyes, and blinked sleepily.

"There's a surprise upstairs," I told her. "God gave us something special last night."

Rachel sat up as she tried to grasp what I was telling her.

"We have a *baby*, a tiny baby sister!" I said.

Her eyes opened wide now, and Rachel threw her arms around my neck. "Take me up. I want to see her."

I picked her up and held her close to me as I headed up the stairs. Her warm body was shaking with excitement.

"There's the baby!" I announced. I set Rachel down in front of Rebecca, who was cuddling little Esther Marie at the moment.

Rachel had wonder and delight on her face as she looked up at me and said simply, "I like her."

"We all love her," I said. "We're so glad God gave her to us."

Rachel nodded her tousled head vigorously.

A Precious Sunbeam

Joanna Yoder

*Lo, children are an heritage of the LORD: and the
fruit of the womb is his reward (Psalm 127:3).*

WHAT ARE YOU DOING TODAY?" I ASKED MOM ONE FRIDAY MORNING
as I helped her clear the breakfast table. Our darling little sister, four-
year-old Esther Marie, was still in bed.

"I'd really like to finish Esther Marie's dress before Sunday," Mother
replied. "And this afternoon Dad wants me to clean his office. In the
meantime Anna Mary can help with the laundry."

I heard Esther Marie's voice call from the basement bedroom, and
Mom hurried down to return with our tousle-headed little sister. It had
been four-and-a-half years since the memorable night when Esther
Marie was born. She was now a lively, brown-eyed girl.

"I want chocolate milk and stories," Esther Marie announced.

So Mom and Esther Marie were soon settled down with a story-
book as Anna Mary began to sort the dry laundry off the lines in the
basement. We hang the wash indoors in cold weather and it takes
longer than a day to dry sometimes. When Anna Mary brought the dry
wash up, I put away the shirts and dresses first and then folded a large
pile of towels. A family of nine sure makes a lot of laundry.

Esther Marie now sat on the floor with her head bent over a piece
of paper, drawing. I paused to look. "What are you making?"

"It's Anna Mary," Esther Marie said. "She's screaming because a
bear is coming." Esther Marie pointed to a scraggly animal with a big
mouth. Her finger continued on. "And this is me. I'm running to the
house." Her quick finger drew another woman with outstretched arms.
"This is Mom coming to save Anna Mary."

"You're quite the artist," I laughed.

"What's an artist?" Esther Marie asked. But she didn't wait for an answer, and I glanced at the clock. It was 11:30. Mom was busy at the sewing machine, so I needed to get busy with lunch. Did we have any leftovers from supper?

We didn't, so I ran down the basement stairs and entered the can room. The floor felt cool to my stockinged feet and I breathed the delicious air deeply. I strained to see in the semidarkness and searched the shelves laden with canned fruits, vegetables, and meat. Ah…there it was. I grabbed a jar of soup and stepped around a pail of carrots as I hurried back to the kitchen.

"What are you making?" Esther Marie asked as I dumped the soup into a kettle.

"Tomato soup," I answered. "Does that sound good?"

"I want a toasted cheese sandwich," she responded.

"That would go well with the soup," I agreed. "Can you place the silverware on the table for me?"

Esther Marie did so without complaint, and half an hour later our enjoyable lunch was finished. I ran water in the sink and added a squirt of soap in preparation for dish washing.

"Who can play with me?" Esther Marie pleaded.

"I have to wash dishes," I said. "Why don't you go ask Mom what you can do?"

She disappeared, but returned a few minutes later. "I want to play at washing laundry, and Mom said you could make lines for me."

So I stopped work and strung yarn across the living room. Esther Marie soon had her doll clothing ready for her pretend washing machine and the pretend water. She proceeded to hang her doll clothing on the yarn lines.

I returned to the dishes and sang to entertain myself. Mom soon left for the trip over to Dad's workplace to clean and Esther Marie again begged for someone to play with her.

"Why don't you put your puzzles together?" I said. "That would give you something to do."

She hesitated a moment, so I helped gather them up and soon she was settled on the kitchen floor close to me, chattering as she played. "I'm going to do the ABC puzzle first. But what is this?" She held up the piece.

"That's a Q, as in queen," I answered.

"I'm going to do the cow puzzle now," Esther Marie soon announced.

"Mom and Dad gave me that puzzle when I was five," I said. Then I pointed to a puzzle of wild animals. "We got that when we went to the zoo."

"Tell me a story about when you were a little girl." Her eyes sparkled with anticipation.

"One time when I was about five," I began, "I went on a trip without Mom and Dad. Aunt Clara Beth was along, though. We started out early one morning…"

After that story she begged for another one, and another one.

"I'm about tired of stories," I said. "Why don't you tell me a story about when you were a little girl?"

"But you know all my stories already," she protested.

I knelt by her on the floor. "I have an idea. Tonight I plan to attend a youth gathering. While I'm gone, why don't you remember what happens and when I come home, you can tell me everything."

She was excited about the plan, and the day continued. Wilma and Rachel arrived home from school and I fixed them a snack. Since Esther Marie wanted to play again, Anna Mary helped her wrap up our little dog, Kobe, in a blanket, and they soon had him sitting helplessly in the doll stroller.

I settled on a chair to mend one of my dresses, but couldn't find the patch. Esther Marie noticed my search and pulled the piece out of her pocket. I laughed and gave her a hug. Little sisters surely keep life interesting. It was now close to supper time and I rushed about to get ready for the evening's youth gathering.

"What time do we leave?" I asked my brother, Titus.

"No later than twenty past six," he said.

So after a quick supper we left for the mile-and-a-half trip. All of the young people were soon busy on various projects. We split and stacked wood that evening and did small construction jobs. By nine we all gathered at the house for a snack.

After the prayer, I relaxed and visited with the other girls as we ate crackers with cheese and ham. Before long Titus motioned from the doorway that he was ready to leave. I hurried to get my coat and bonnet. At home I wondered if Esther Marie would remember her assignment.

As I entered the basement, a small figure darted out of the little girl's bedroom. Esther Marie flung her arms around my legs, so I took off my outer wraps and sat on the edge of her bed. She climbed into my lap.

"Now tell me what you did tonight," I said as she cuddled against me. I could feel the softness of her pink nightgown and smell the scent of shampoo in her hair.

Esther Marie bounced on my knee. "First of all I had stories. Next Mom helped me and Rachel play I-Spy. Then she read our Bible story. After that Dad prayed, and we went to bed."

I laughed. Her story had been short, but it wasn't hard to imagine the many details she hadn't mentioned.

"That sounds like fun," I told her. "Did you have a snack after the Bible story and prayer?"

"A cookie." She bounced again.

"Did you brush your teeth?"

"Mom helped me. Then I went to bed and saw you come home." She grinned from ear to ear as I tucked her under the covers.

"Night-night," I whispered.

Quietly I left the room and later knelt to pray at my bedside before I crawled in. I added a special prayer that night for my dear little sister, Esther Marie.

High Water

Malinda Hershberger

*I had fainted, unless I had believed to see the goodness
of the LORD in the land of the living (Psalm 27:13).*

AN UNUSUAL HAPPENING OCCURRED IN JANUARY OF 2005, AFTER MY husband, Reuben, and I had been married nearly a year. On this particular Friday evening we were driving toward my parents' house with plans to stay for the night. My two married siblings, plus Reuben and I, wanted to help with the hog butchering the next day.

I had baked pies and made a large pan of pineapple delight pudding in preparation. Those were now under the buggy seat, along with a handbag containing several butchering knives, a wallet with cash, a book, a stone crock with a plastic lid, and some other items. We planned to stop in at the Family Dollar store in Brewster and then travel on to my parents' place for supper.

Due to recent heavy rains, there were flooded areas along our route. This wasn't an unusual situation for our area, but normally it didn't get this bad. More than once we had driven through water on this road, so we should have been used to it.

That night as we drove toward town on Harrison Road and darkness was falling, we stopped to light our lanterns when we came to a place where there was a "High Water, Road Closed" sign. I asked Reuben if we'd better leave the lowest lantern off its bracket for fear of its getting wet. But he thought the water wouldn't be that deep.

We drove on and soon came to an area where the water covered the road for a pretty long stretch. It didn't look deep, but we knew looks could be deceiving. The water makes it look as though the road is level, whereas it often dips. We knew that much, but what we didn't know was that ahead of us lay a length of road with two mailboxes covered in water.

We also knew from experience that horses and buggies can get through places motor vehicles can't. Reuben now pulled back on the reins, feeling reluctant to go on, but I urged him to drive on.

Our horse Mabel took to the water nicely. She was a well-liked horse and a good traveler. Her only drawback was that she didn't like to back up. We would try sometimes, but we rarely succeeded.

Now, as we drove in further, we noticed the water was rising a bit. Thankfully this wasn't running water; it was backup from the Beach City Dam, and was almost at a standstill.

Suddenly Mabel jumped. Apparently she stepped into the ditch or a washout.

"The road's washed out," Reuben muttered.

Mabel was struggling in the water, dragging the buggy with her until the two front wheels dropped in the hole. Reuben was standing on the dashboard and I was at the side door, with both of our heads thankfully out of the water.

Reuben told me to jump and to keep clear from the thrashing Mabel, but I couldn't. Rueben then climbed up on top of the buggy and helped me up. It was too dangerous for him to try to cut Mabel loose. We sat there, watching Mabel's thrashing eventually die down. We knew she was dead. I would have expected great waves of grief to overwhelm me to see our precious horse die in front of our eyes, but I first felt relief that her sufferings were over so quickly. It had been an agony to watch her struggle so. And if it had gone on much longer the buggy would have tipped over with us on it.

Mabel had vanished completely under the water, leaving only ripples of foam floating above her. What a cruel way indeed for someone to kill their horse. We hadn't intended it, of course, but Mabel's death still tore at our hearts. We should never have put our horse in that kind of danger.

With Mabel gone we turned our attention to our own survival. Would we now have to rescue ourselves? Little did we realize at the time what a large protecting Hand was watching over us.

I guess I was more shaken up than I realized at the time. I asked Reuben if he thought a helicopter would come get us. I think he was trying to comfort me by saying it probably would.

Before we had climbed on top of the buggy, Reuben had already given out a cry for help. Unbeknownst to us, an *English* man named Mark had heard us. He proceeded to jump into his neighbor's flat-bottom boat and use its one oar to row out to us. He told us later that his own lane and mailbox were also under water. His wife had arrived home as Mark set out in the boat, and she had to turn into someone else's driveway. Mark called over to her, telling his wife to back the car down to the water's edge and turn the heat on.

This was, after all, January weather, and we were sitting soaking wet on top of a buggy. I was getting stiff and sore, to say the least. The front of the buggy top was almost down to the surface of the water with about a foot of the back stuck out. Mark, the *English* man, rowed the boat toward us, docking carefully, and we got in. He took us to where his wife had the car waiting and we climbed inside where it was warm. It had been a long time since anything had felt so good.

We thanked Mark profusely, but he brushed it off, telling his wife to take us back to our home, which she did.

When we were inside our house, we discarded our wet clothes and I took a hot bath, which I figured was the best way to continue warming up. By the time we were ready for supper, Reuben had lost his appetite thinking about the accident and Mabel. Sleep didn't come easily for either of us that night.

We were awakened in the middle of the night by knocking on the front door. The sheriff and Mark were outside. Mark hadn't reported the accident until he realized that divers had been called in to search the area around the buggy. The sheriff wouldn't take his word though, that we had survived. Which was why he was there to speak with us in person.

The following morning we took our old buggy and our other driving horse, setting out for my parents again. We detoured around two flooded areas, not including the one with Mabel and our buggy still in it.

That evening after the butchering was finished, some of the family and Reuben decided to borrow a boat and try to bring Mabel and the buggy out. Of course I went along, not wanting to stay behind. Thankfully they didn't have that difficult a task. They pulled poor Mabel out with the buggy dragging behind her.

I poured the water out of the pie and pudding, but they were of course not salvageable. The crock pot and plastic lid had floated away. Everything else though, was still there. Our buggy robe was lying beside the road. I took it home and washed it. Except for small holes in the outer lining, it's still used today. We put the buggy in a neighbor's shop to dry and are still using it.

I know we would never have driven into that water if we had known it was so deep. Then our faithful Mabel wouldn't have been lost. I guess God had a reason for sparing our lives. We certainly learned a lesson through the experience. One we hopefully will never forget. Never keep driving when you come upon a sign that says "High Water, Road Closed."

Kerlin

Eldon Schrock

Who knoweth the spirit of man that goeth upward, and the spirit of the beast that goeth downward to the earth? (Ecclesiastes 3:21).

WHEN I WAS 17, MY DAD AND BROTHER DUANE STARTED ITCHING TO have some sheep. We had wanted some for a long time, and one day we heard, much to our delight, that our coworker, Jake, wanted to sell his small flock of six American Blackbelly sheep.

Jake told us these sheep were very hardy and that they never had lambing problems. They have hair instead of wool, which meant we wouldn't have to shear them. We decided we couldn't go wrong. The next Saturday we brought them home. The truckload consisted of a large ram, two ewes, and three lambs. We named the ram Kerlin.

Three months into our fledgling business, Kerlin started losing weight. Soon he was obviously quite sick. Dad purchased medicine for him, but Kerlin continued to get worse. Finally one evening, he couldn't even get to his feet.

Duane and I ran to inform Dad, who told us, "Call Jake right away." Jake had lots of experience with sheep. He'd know what to do.

I headed for the phone shack and called Jake. He listened to my description of our troubles and suggested, "You should give him penicillin."

"We don't have any," I said.

"I'll bring mine in the morning when I come to work," Jake replied in his usual neighborly fashion.

I thanked him and hung up. The next morning, the minute breakfast was over, I left for our home business where we build propane refrigerators. Jake arrived soon after I did and handed me the bottle of penicillin.

"Here's what you've been looking for," Jake told me with a big smile. "Oh, and by the way, you should probably also call the vet," he added.

I was ready to rush back to Kerlin when I remembered I didn't know how to inject penicillin in a sheep or how much to give.

"Your dad will know. He's raised a lot of calves," Jake said.

"Thanks," I said, racing back to our barn. I found Dad and told him what Jake had said.

We rushed out to the barn where poor Kerlin lay. We helped him to his feet. Dad gave the injection and left Kerlin food and water in hopes that he would soon be well. Kerlin did try to drink from the bucket and stared at us afterward with unblinking eyes.

"Check on him at first break," Dad instructed me, and I did so, finding Kerlin much the same, though he had managed to drag himself around his box stall some. *Well*, I thought, *I'll go back to work, and I'll call the vet too. Maybe he'll have some more ideas.* I went to the phone shack and got out the phone book. I flipped to the Yellow Pages and looked under *Veterinarians*. My finger traced down the list. There it was. I dialed the number.

A cheery voice answered and I explained, "This is Eldon Shrock calling from over here by Evart. I have a sick ram that needs some help and I was wondering if I could speak to a veterinarian."

"You said a sick ram?" the woman asked.

"Yes," I answered.

"Then you need to speak to Dr. Miller. Hang on a minute."

She put me on hold and soon a man's voice came on the line. "Dr. Miller. How can I help you?"

"This is Eldon Shrock calling from over here by Evart," I repeated. "I have a sick ram that has been losing weight. He also has some problems standing. We help him to his feet, but a minute later he lies down again. We started giving him penicillin this morning, and I was wondering if there is anything else we should be doing."

"Well…sounds like you're doing the right thing," Dr. Miller said. "I don't know what else to suggest right now. If he gets worse in the next few days, give me a call back."

I hung up and went back home. But Kerlin remained unchanged for the next few days. Finally we decided he should go outside and get some fresh air. However, *where* was the question. We didn't want him in the front yard where he wouldn't get the shade he needed, since it was quite warm. We eventually came up with the idea of taking the round bale feeder and covering it with plywood behind the barn to give him some shade.

The following day we built our Kerlin shelter. When we finished, the next problem was transporting Kerlin to his new home.

"We couldn't carry him," I said.

"Let's use the wagon," Duane suggested.

I agreed, so we put cardboard on the red wagon to protect Kerlin from splinters, since the wagon was made of wood and was very old. With one of us taking the front half of Kerlin and the other the rear half, we loaded him on for his ride. What a sight we made with this stately ram on the old red wagon looking very uncomfortable. My sisters laughed at us as we took off toward the shelter. I pulled the wagon slowly so Kerlin wouldn't get a bumpy ride. Around the barn and out into the field we went. Nonetheless, we arrived safely with me pulling the wagon and Duane supporting Kerlin so he wouldn't fall off.

We unloaded him and got him inside the shelter. Everyone pitched in to pick fresh grass for him, and we supplied him with plenty of water. Then back to work we went, with the thought of Kerlin in the back of our minds.

I went to check on him later in the day. As I came close to the shelter, there was no Kerlin in sight. I did a quick search and found him a distance away under a tree where he had dragged himself.

Wow, I thought. *He can't get up but he can really drag himself around.* I called Duane to help me get him into the pen again, where I refilled his water bucket and picked more fresh grass.

That evening Duane and I tended to Kerlin again. We had high hopes, but by the next morning there were no signs of improvement. If anything, Kerlin was worse. Duane and I consulted with each other on our next course of action and also asked Dad. At his suggestion, we called the vet. He said Kerlin might have *coccidiosis,* and prescribed corid and some thick pasty stuff that was supposed to give Kerlin more energy to help him fight the sickness. Dad called a local taxi driver and went into Reed City to the vet's store. There he picked up the prescriptions.

We gave Kerlin the medicine that evening, but by the next morning he was worse than ever. Dad came over to try his hand at giving Kerlin his medicine, and later that morning I went back to check on Kerlin. As I got closer he didn't move his eyes at all. Then I looked at his stomach and saw that he wasn't breathing. Kerlin had died.

I immediately called Dad and Duane, telling them the sad news.

After work Duane and I loaded Kerlin and hooked the wagon to the walk-behind mower. I carefully drove the mower out behind the barn by the fencerow to where we had a few apple trees that were in full blossom. Underneath the largest and prettiest one, we dug a fair-sized grave, digging deep enough so no coyotes or wild dogs would dig him up.

Then we placed our prized ram, the one that showed so much promise, into the grave and covered him in dirt. That was a sorrowful day for all of us. Thankfully we had two attractive little rams who soon grew up so we could keep on adding to our flock. We comforted ourselves and looked forward to better days ahead.

Billy Goat Style

Oba Hershberger

*A merry heart doeth good like a medicine: but a
broken spirit drieth the bones (Proverbs 17:22).*

MY BROTHER-IN-LAW LEVI YODER WAS PREACHING ONE DAY ON THE subject of sheep and goats. Now, of course, he said, we should all be like sheep, easily led and meek. Then Levi added that it's hard to teach a goat something and to make them remember.

Now, isn't that the truth!

The following Monday I was pondering these truths, and of course my mind has a habit of wandering. I get so far afield that it sometimes gets tangled up in other stuff. In my thinking that day I was wishing that Levi had warned me 50 years ago about those goats, because it sure could have saved me some grief. See, back a long time ago, I had a habit of trying to drive anything that had four legs.

Now our family dog wasn't hard to train, and I had hours of fun with him. Then for some reason, which I no longer can remember, Dad bought me two little billy goats at the sale barn. They were for me to play with, he said. I was the youngest, and he probably thought this was cheaper than another brother or sister, since I was child number 14. So I took to those two little rascals. I named them Dick and Din and watched them grow.

Now it was hard to make pets out of animals who got beat over the head by Mom and my sisters every time they ventured into the flower beds. The goats eventually got soured at the whole human race. But one lesson I learned from this time in my life was how to mediate between females and goats.

The day arrived when I created a harness for the two goats. Of course there was some twine and baling wire involved. Next I took my little two-wheeled cart that I had made for the dog and put in a tongue instead of shafts.

Now, I'll be the first to admit that I'm not much of a genius at harness making or cart crafting. I'm aware that my services in designing machinery were never sought after by Wayne Wengerd or White Horse Machine.

But I wasn't disheartened. I set to work, and the great day finally arrived. My chariot was ready. The goats were pretty gentle by this time, or so I thought. I had been driving them together with nothing hitched behind them, so at this point I figured all was well.

One evening I got the goats all ready to hook up right after the chores. Out in front of the barn I had my sister Mary hold them while I did the real important stuff, like getting the tongue of the cart between them.

Also I should mention that at this time of the night, if you had driven by our old homestead, you might have noticed big white geese walking out toward the barn on their way to eat a little cow feed that was left scattered there. I should also mention that we all knew goats and geese didn't mix.

Sister Mary was getting mighty squeamish by now, trying to hang on to those fine specimens called goats. But I was like the other younger boys, thinking my sisters were sissies. So I continued and got the goats hitched up. I got in my chariot and grabbed the lines. Dick and Din took off at a mighty fine trot. I imagined they even paced, but it might have been a gallop. I really couldn't remember much afterward about those particular moments.

The evening was windy, and I didn't have any elastic band under my chin to keep my derby on my noggin. And let me tell you, this little flying Dutchman was getting the ride of his life.

Then we met the aforementioned geese. My hat flew off in the general direction of the geese, landing on one of them—or so they say. Business really picked up after that, as geese make very funny noises when excited.

Well, in all that fuss, the geese went one way and the goats went another. Of course there was still some direction not used yet. And you guessed it. That direction was up! I took that route when we hit the walks. And if one goes up, one usually comes down again. Which I did. When I landed in the dust, I had also been left behind as the goats continued on.

I wish this story would end with the hero riding off into the sunset, but it doesn't. The goats ran into my shop. My shop with a door that was approximately 36 inches wide while the width of my chariot measured 48 inches. That might not sound like much of a difference between the door and the chariot, but I can assure you it is.

When those two objects met each other, all of my fine workmanship came to naught. Harness parts, or might I say twine, leather, wire, wheels, axles, tongue, seat, and other assorted items too numerous to mention, were all sadly scattered.

When I limped into the shop, there Dick and Din stood at the top of the shop stairway looking at me with those mournful eyes. And all they said was, "Ba-a-a."

Our New Life Together

Oba Hershberger

The wicked flee when no man pursueth: but the
righteous are bold as a lion (Proverbs 28:1).

On November 7, 1968, something took place that had never happened to me before. My uncle, Bishop John, placed a woman's hand in mine and somehow or other we were married. I'm pretty sure we said "yes" to all the questions he asked us. But at the time I was so nervous I'm not sure what those questions were. If the bishop had asked me if I'd promise to wash the dishes every day, I'm sure I would have agreed.

We soon set up house in an old farmhouse. My good wife, Lorene, wasn't a complainer, so we made it through that first winter with flying colors. Though we did discover that the old house was a lot easier to keep warm in the summer than in the winter.

I had been a farmer's boy growing up, and that was what I liked. But my dad had retired from farming in 1963 and one of my brothers-in-law, Andy Yoder, had taken over the farm. I, being the youngest in our tribe of 14, started working in the carpenter trade.

Now let me be the first to tell you that I was not a carpenter at heart. But my new wife just didn't have enough work for me in the kitchen, so I figured I'd better keep my job. At the time I was paid $2.35 an hour, which was second to the top wage our boss was paying. He had around 40 men working for him. I was on his framing crew under my brother Monroe, who was the foreman.

The eight of us working under Monroe had a lot of fun, but Lorene and I both wanted to farm instead, which would give us more time together. But no farms were available at that time, so we kept on saving our money and praying. We also had hope invested in my dad, knowing that in the past he had helped others of our family get on a farm. He'd even help with building if there was a need.

So we couldn't have been happier when Dad stopped at our place one evening in the fall of 1969 and told us Ben Kuhn's farm might be for rent. Whoopee! But there was one kicker. The farm was about 14 miles south of where we lived. It also had old buildings and an old house. But Amish farmers had been renting the place for many years, so it was ready to go as a 200-acre dairy farm.

Our closest Amish neighbors would be Jake and Mary Otto, the parents of an only child, Big John Otto. This old place also had a mile-long lane. But all that didn't discourage us. We were so excited about moving onto a dairy farm that nothing was going to dampen our enthusiasm.

So in October of 1969 we started milking cows and feeding a few hogs. When I look back and realize how little I knew and how much I needed to learn, it about makes my knees shake.

Our long lane had a few drawbacks, one of them being that people would drive up the lane right to our house at night, thinking it was a road. I never was the bravest Indian in the tribe, so I'd sigh with relief when the car turned around and went right back out the lane.

A nice feature of the farm was the river running along the edge with lots of woods behind it. The woods, though, were owned by a non-Amish neighbor. Sometimes folks would park their trucks near our house to hunt coon in those woods. Now that would really get us skittish. We might be in bed, and here comes a slow-moving truck into our lane. They'd park near the house. And what were we to think? Did a kidnapping lie ahead of us? But we tried to remain calm while we figured out who this might be.

In January we had an incident I'll never forget. We'd finished the chores, eaten supper, and gone to bed. I can't remember what we had for supper, but I'm sure it was good. I'd discovered by this time that not only was my wife, Lorene, the prettiest lady in Coles, Moultrie, Douglas, and other surrounding counties, but she was also the best cook.

Anyway, lying there in bed, we heard a bang somewhere near the kitchen. Lorene whispered, "There's a commotion going on out there."

Well, I was trying to listen, but my heart and my knees weren't quite working together, so I couldn't hear too well. Then the noise really picked up. I told myself I mustn't act scared for my good wife's sake.

I slowly got out of bed. The moon was supplying me with enough light to dress by. Of course my fingers were scared. They didn't want to get ahold of those buttons, but I got them calmed down. But here was the real sticker: By this time the racket was quite lively, and my knees weren't behaving again.

As I was leaving the bedroom in this condition, my dear wife was faced with a dilemma. What was she to do? She didn't want to stay in the bedroom by herself. But she also didn't want to get in my way, in case I'd have to run real fast toward this racket. So she consulted with me in whispers and took my hand—I can still remember how firmly she grasped it. It brought tears to my eyes, how trusting women can be.

We crept into the living room together, our flashlights in hand. We eased our way into the kitchen and the noise was still going on. We could now tell it was coming from the porch.

My poor heart still pounds today when I think of that moment when I slid back the curtain and shone my flashlight out there. This is also the embarrassing part. See, a few days earlier my wife had set a wooden mousetrap on the porch. I could of course say that a big panther had snuck in and caught its paw, but that wouldn't be true. Instead, I have to admit that it was a mouse making all that racket. He had somehow fastened his tail in my wife's trap and that trap was going as fast as that little rodent could trot.

About then the good wife recalled that she'd read somewhere in a book on marriage that the man of the house is supposed to take charge when things get a little tough. She seemed to think this came under that heading. So with me still being in the first year of marriage, I did want to impress her with my bravery.

I sized up the situation and told her the first order of this operation was for her to keep her flashlight trained on the mouse. I'd then grab the thing and go from there.

Well…it turned out to be quite a chase. Soon both the mouse and I desired a break, but there was no coffee handy. So we continued to play cat and mouse, with me as the cat. When I went a little faster, my fine little friend also increased his speed.

But as all good things do, this too came to an end. And all parties were happy with the outcome, except perhaps the one in the trap. He left a piece of his tail behind. Now there is a dock-tailed mouse running around somewhere, unless he died of old age or a heart attack. I, on my part, tried to avoid that affliction by heading back to bed. We figured that was enough excitement for a while.

The Pig Chase
Sarah Bontrager

*A time to love, and a time to hate; a time of
war, and a time of peace (Ecclesiastes 3:8).*

I WAS 16 AND HUMMING SOFTLY TO MYSELF AS I AMBLED TO THE
chicken house that evening to gather eggs. Next, I'd weed the strawberry patch with Mom and my four younger siblings. Supper needed
to be prepared too, but with Dad gone to a minister's meeting, com-
pleting the chores had fallen on our shoulders.

We had put hay in the hay feeders for all the horses and our beef
cows. We had milked the Jersey cow and filled the water dishes of the
two Pomeranian dogs that shared our place with a dozen cats. The
chickens had been fed earlier, as had our two piglets.

What a beautiful evening, I thought. *If only Dad could be home to
enjoy our family time together.* But I knew he was on a worthwhile mis-
sion, taking care of church work.

My thoughts were interrupted by someone shouting, "Your pigs
are out! Your pigs are out!"

I turned to see our neighbors Henry and Edna running through the
orchard following our two squealing piglets.

Oh, no, I thought. *I must go find more help.* And with that I flung
my pail and raced for the house.

Bursting through the screen door I yelled, "Mom! Girls! Our two
piglets are out!"

"No!" Mom exclaimed. "Come, let's hurry before they find the garden and ruin our vegetables."

We hurried outside to find Henry and Edna gone. We figured they
had returned home. We knew they couldn't leave their two-year-old

daughter unattended. We didn't know that Henry also went looking for his net with which he planned to catch the piglets.

As we charged around the corner of our implements shed, we almost fell on top of the two piglets. They squealed in fright and the race was on.

"Oh…I wish Dad was home to help us!" my sister Mary gasped.

But in a few minutes we had the two piglets cornered and heading in the direction of the pig shed. Or so we thought.

"This will be easy," I said to the others. "We'll open the door of the pig shed. Jacob, you stand behind the door to slam it shut as soon as they're inside. The rest of us will continue chasing them in."

Eight-year-old Jacob nodded and moments later there was a horrible mess of flailing arms and yelling girls mixed in with squealing pigs. Those pigs went everywhere but the doorway. We'd catch our breath and try the whole thing all over again…only to have them escape again. We couldn't even stop them when they dashed between our legs. All that resulted was our own upending into the dirt as the pigs ran off, squealing in double fright.

Finally we gave up. "This isn't working," I panted. "There must be some other way to get them back in!"

"Indeed," agreed Anna. "This is ridiculous. All we're doing is running around in circles. Maybe we could just grab them and carry them in."

"I doubt if that would work." I continued to gasp for air.

"We have nothing to lose," Ruth said, all brave and bold.

"Anything's better than this," Anna said. "I'm surprised my dress is still in one piece."

As my breath came in shorter gasps I considered their plan. "I suppose those pigs really are small enough to carry," I finally agreed.

So we set out with Anna muttering under her breath, "Okay, piggies, here we come again."

By now the two runaways had discovered our woodshed and were rooting around in the loose dirt and bark. We heard satisfied little grunts coming from inside.

With fresh zest, I charged after them and actually got one cornered.

I pounced, landing on top of her. What a squealing fit there was with those pig legs kicking furiously. I wrapped my arms tightly around her belly and gleefully ran toward the pigpen. I lifted her above the hog panels and set her down inside. At last! One down! Now the next one!

I turned to hear Anna yell. "Help me! I caught her!"

Quickly I ran to Anna's aid and together we tried desperately to keep a hold on the pig. This time it wasn't working. Gradually we were losing our grip and soon the pig was free again. It took off hightailing it in the opposite direction.

I sat in the dirt in near tears. "This is hopeless. It's going to take all evening."

The other girls ignored me and raced off after the pig. I gathered my wits and followed them. By the time I reached them, they had the pig cornered. Seeing me, the pig made for its escape. This time I dived at the animal and grabbed its belly with both arms. And I hung on. I couldn't keep a good grip, though. This pig was obviously heavier than the other one.

It rolled and kicked, dirt flying in my face. I was down to a hold on one leg. I remember being scared the leg might come off. But whoever heard of such a thing? I was now on my stomach being dragged along. Thankfully Anna got her arm around the pig's stomach, and the now-tired animal calmed down enough that we could carry her to the pen.

We all stood there panting. Ruth quickly placed a board in front of the tiny hole where they had escaped.

"There. That'll do until Dad gets it fixed," she said, adding a cement block in front of the board for good measure.

I stood there brushing dust from my cape and apron. One of my covering strings was torn off. The head covering itself was dirt-covered and smashed. Quite unladylike, I figured. And to make things worse there were peals of laughter behind us. Henry and Edna had returned. Edna had their two-year-old in her arms and Henry had his net.

"Are you okay?" Edna asked between her giggles.

"I'm not hurt," I said, perhaps sounding a bit shorter with her than I should. My face was scarlet red and covered with brown smudges. At the moment, I didn't find any of this amusing.

"I'm sorry for laughing," Edna apologized at once.

Henry, of course, didn't say he was sorry. "Maybe someday you can look back and laugh about your first pig chase," he said, still grinning.

"Why didn't you bring your net earlier?" I asked Henry, trying to collect myself.

"I couldn't find it," Henry said. "It was stuck in the darkest corner of our buggy shed."

"That's okay," I said, feeling sheepish now. "I guess it doesn't help being upset about this."

Jacob now jumped in with his own question for Henry. "How did you discover the pigs were out?"

Henry grinned again. "Oh…it was so cute! We heard these funny noises in the backyard and went out on the porch to investigate. It took a while until we saw their snooty faces peeping over the tall grass."

"We stood there laughing for a few seconds," Edna added.

"All's well that ends well," Mom announced. She had climbed up on the manure spreader seat and maintained her perch the whole time the ruckus was going on. "I guess we learned something tonight we wouldn't have by weeding the strawberry patch."

"And we made more memories!" declared Jacob.

We all laughed heartily, including myself.

"Here comes Dad!" exclaimed Mary.

And with that she and Jacob bolted for the buggy coming in our driveway. They hopped alongside the buggy's open door, excitedly telling Dad all about the extraordinary event of the evening.

"Whoa!" Dad said as they arrived at the buggy shed. "I'm sorry I missed out on the show. Sounds like some great sightseeing!"

The rest of us agreed, and a jolly group trooped back into the house at long last to clean up and prepare for supper.

Why Don't We Butcher?

Aaron Miller

*And they that shall be of thee shall build the old waste
places: thou shalt raise up the foundations of many
generations; and thou shalt be called, The repairer of the
breach, The restorer of paths to dwell in (Isaiah 58:12).*

IT WAS AN INNOCENT STATEMENT I UTTERED THAT DAY TO MY BROTHER
David. "We're almost out of meat in our freezer. Why don't we butcher?"
All I was trying to do, I suppose, was revive a family tradition.

There was of course Valley Meats and Yoder's Custom Meats and
the other meat processing places not far away. But the thought of doing
our own butchering had always fascinated me. I saw gleaming stainless
steel knives in my mind's eye, tables heavily laden at the end of the day
with neatly packaged meat ready for the freezer, long coils of sausage
ready for canning, and the enjoyment of eating it all later. Oh, yeah, I
had it all pictured the way it *should* happen.

I now know that this is the kind of thing one imagines when you
don't have a lot of experience with butchering. Or, for instance, the
knowledge that your meat grinder is a sadistic machine that loves to
create problems. Or that your sausage stuffer has internal issues. I
had yet to learn that those are all things that can happen when you
get together on a snowy afternoon and try to accomplish something
worthwhile.

From the get-go, David and I struggled to find a date that would
accommodate both of our busy families. Dates were set and reset.
Finally we settled on Friday, February 22, as the day we'd gather on my
brother's farm in the hills of Holmes County for this important event.

When we arrived, several of the butchers were already hard at work
cutting meat from the bones of a large steer. Now I had heard from

others that a butcher cuts the bones out of the meat, and others of lesser talent cut the meat off the bones. I had visions of being in the former category, but at least I knew I wasn't.

Throughout the busy afternoon things went quite well. Everyone was pitching in, and we were soon finished cutting the meat from the bones of both a steer and a hog. I had noticed all afternoon that whenever David spoke of meat grinders, he would add that meat grinders have ruined many a good butchering day. I comforted myself that in our case we had taken care of the problem by planning to borrow a recently repaired grinder. I figured the machine was ready for action.

But I think if we would have been listening we would have heard the meat grinder and sausage stuffer conversing back and forth as the day wore on.

"Just wait until they try to put me together," the grinder was gloating.

"You haven't got anything on me," the stuffer replied. "I'll have them tearing their hair out. They don't have the parts they need, and they don't know where to put the parts they have."

This would have been followed, no doubt, by waves of laughter between the two.

It was around 5:00 when we made our first attempt to put the grinder into action. That attempt, though, was unsuccessful. And of course we all know that men aren't prone to ask for directions, even when they don't know what they're doing.

So we tried again…and again. Hammers pounded. Vise grips gripped. We griped. We sweated and did our best impression of someone who knew what they were doing, trying to get that grinder to grind. We even had backseat drivers who seemed to know a lot more about the grinder than we did.

By now, I began to wonder if our scheduled pickup at 9:00 would be anywhere close to the right time. To make matters more complicated, the snow was coming down hard by now, and the lane at David's is rather steep. It's difficult to traverse in dry conditions. If it's snowy and slippery, things can get ugly in a hurry.

We continued to fight with the grinder, the cold sweat dripping from our foreheads.

Then finally someone succeeded in placing what looked like the right parts in the right place, and the first piece of meat was gently tossed into the hopper. It flopped, hopped, and squished and did about anything it could do except come out the front end resembling hamburger. The backseat drivers were all looking at each other with knowing smirks on their faces. So we gave up, and the trek was made to the neighbor's to obtain another meat grinder.

The time was 7:30 when we actually began grinding our meat. At least grinding with the replacement grinder was pretty pain-free. We soon had our task completed and were bagging and putting our prized hamburger into freezer bags.

The problem was a blizzard had begun blowing outside, and we no longer had a way home. So the decision was made to stay overnight and attempt the trip in the morning.

At least we now had time for a leisurely time spent with the stuffer...or so I thought.

I could already taste the canned sausage with mustard, topped with all the trimmings. The stuffer was supposed to produce foot after foot of wonderful sausage. Borrowed as it was from a good friend of mine, I never doubted its abilities. When I had picked up the stuffer, he had assured me that after talking with his dad, everything we needed to make our day of sausage stuffing a success was included in this little gadget. We were ready to roll, he said.

So the first load of sausage was piled into the little press and the pressing began. Some sausage came rolling out of the tube where it was supposed to, but a large amount came puking out of the sides and over the top of the lid. We pushed and pressed on, proceeding to make sausage.

Our efforts were hampered by a plate at the bottom of the press that kept plugging up, and I'll admit that we should have thought things through and left the plate out after unclogging it several times. But how were we to know the press we were using was set up for pressing out fat instead of sausage?

By now it was 10:00, and I remembered Valley Meats and Yoder's Custom Meats. The vision of their smooth operation kept popping into my tired mind. Finally we all looked at each other and someone said, "Bulk sausage is the way to go. We love sausages on the grill."

So the sausage stuffer was laid to rest in a corner. We did get some stuffed sausage, but a larger portion was headed for jars and the freezer. Our educational and entertaining day of butchering drew to a close at around midnight. The next morning we enjoyed a delicious breakfast of sausage, eggs, and pancakes with all the trimmings. The great thing about this butchering day was that we are enjoying fresh hamburger and pork at home now.

When I think back, hey…a good time was had by all, and we even learned something in the process! Things don't always have to be trouble free to enjoy God's gift of life that He has given us all.

Spokes and Spooks

Regina Bontrager

*They shall bear thee up in their hands, lest thou
dash thy foot against a stone (Psalm 91:12).*

I HEAVED A CONTENTED SIGH AND LEANED BACK AGAINST THE BUGGY seat. My older sister Keturah and I had been pulling weeds from the neighbor's strawberry patch and were now on our way home. My arms ached from all the stretching.

The soothing sound of Lady's hooves on the gravel enhanced my relaxation. Autumn scents filled the air, the colors at their brightest hues. I had enjoyed the busy summer days and warm temperatures, but with winter coming on, I also looked forward to a slower work schedule.

"Well, I wonder how many van loads of Amish came to our garage sale while we were gone?" Keturah wondered aloud as she drew Lady to a halt in front of our gray barn. Mom was hosting a three-day community garage sale in our big shed. She continued, "I'll get Lady in the barn while you take our hoes and pails off the buggy."

"Sure!" I agreed.

But before I could step out of the buggy, Keturah shouted, "Whoa, Lady! Whoa!"

Lady had gotten spooked. She started to run forward with one of the harness snaps still fastened to the buggy. The harness pulled back across her rump as she took off. Lady panicked and tried to escape what she thought was a crawly creature on her back.

Keturah acted quickly, grabbing for the bridle. "Whoa, Lady! Easy now!" Keturah tried to calm down the horse in reassuring tones.

Still inside the buggy, my eyes were getting bigger as I watched the action outside. Knowing Lady was a nervous horse, I realized I should get out of the buggy right away. But before I could do so, Lady started going in circles, slowly at first, then faster and faster. Keturah still hung on to the lead strap, yelling, "Whoa!" but to no avail.

Anxious to get out of the buggy, I ventured out onto the step and *bang*! Lady turned sharply, causing the buggy to overturn. I was thrown to the ground and landed hard under the buggy, hitting my head.

"Ohhhh!" I yelled in pain, seeing stars. I lifted the buggy off my head and crawled out from beneath.

In the meantime, Lady's lunging and twisting had torn her harness free. Keturah let go of her, turning quickly toward me when she heard me cry out.

By then I had managed to get to the barn, where I collapsed beside the water hydrant with a loud moan. Completely forgetting about Lady, Keturah raced to where I lay. Kneeling beside me, she anxiously asked, "Regina! Are you okay? Are you alive?"

"I don't know," I finally responded in a weak voice.

"You'll be okay! You'll be fine!" Keturah kept telling me. She was trying to reassure me, and also her own doubts, I suppose. I know her words helped me relax.

"Where are you hurting?" Keturah asked. "There where your hand is?"

I moaned as tears ran down my cheeks. I couldn't speak because of the intense pain. My head throbbed as if a hammer was pounding on it. "Ohhhh…!" was all the sound I could make.

Keturah, determined to find the source of pain, peeled away my hand from my scalp. "Oh!" She jerked back, then quickly did her best to appear normal, all the while saying, "Regina, don't move! Stay where you are! I'll go get Mom!"

Not move? I asked myself. Where did she think I would go? Was I okay? That was the important question. I felt suddenly very scared and I sat up. Was I dying? It hurt terribly, but I was still conscious. That was a good sign.

Then I saw a patch of blood on the cement where my head had been. Was I bleeding to death? I felt warm trails of blood trickle down my face. My hand cautiously approached and touched the soft bulge on my scalp.

Keturah had told me I'd be okay, but how could she know? My thoughts raced. The way Keturah had jumped up and fled for the house made me feel like I was already living on borrowed time. For all I knew, I might be dying. Another mighty blast of pain shot through me. "Oh!" I muttered as I weakly lay down again.

More pangs hit sharply. Time and again, I almost passed out. Where was the help? I screamed as the pain became unbearable. Terrified voices soon broke into my wails. "Regina! What's wrong?"

I peered out from under my arm to see my friend Eunice standing there with a worried look. Her little niece Lois stood beside her, now crying at the sight of my bloody face. They had come to buy eggs and had been drawn to my screaming. I kept on wailing as if I hadn't heard them.

Eunice, seeing that I was breathing and conscious, started running toward the house for help. Just then Mom and my four siblings burst out the door and ran toward me.

"Regina! Regina! Are you okay?" Mom kept calling. "Children, step back so I can get a better look." Mom took charge, speaking to me soothingly as she washed away the blood. "Oh good. It isn't bleeding anymore," she said. "Relax, relax, relax. That will help a lot."

"Dad's home!" The cry rang out as Dad rode in the driveway on his bicycle, returning from his school teaching job. The scene that met him must have been astounding. The whole family on practically one spot by the barn, the neighbor ladies standing off to the side, and the flipped buggy on the other. Bits of harness were strewn in the driveway. And one of the girls had tied the half-harnessed Lady to the hitching post.

Dad had all the information he needed by the time he was off his bicycle.

"I'm going to call Pat," he said, "and see if he can take us to the emergency room to check this out." Dad disappeared into the shed where our phone was kept. Pat was a local taxi driver for the Amish. We often hired him when we had to travel distances farther than our horse could handle.

Meanwhile the others helped clean me and prepare me for the trip.

A dark blue head veiling was brought out since the white starched cap was now dirty and dented, with one string torn off. My bare feet were put into Crocs just as Pat came bouncing up the driveway with his truck.

I walked with jittery steps over to the truck and climbed in, with Mom right at my side supporting my head. Dad hopped into the front on the passenger's side, and off we zoomed to the hospital.

The visit to the ER stretched into two hours as they cleaned and checked out the bump on my scalp.

"Well…it looks like a slight concussion and a bad road burn," the nurse told us. "The X-rays showed no internal bleeding, so you should be fine soon. Here's some medication for the pain, and for the first week you should rest a lot."

"What a relief it isn't worse!" I remarked to my parents. "I already feel better." I rejoiced as the nurse bandaged my scalp.

So I spent time on my back the next week as I waited for my head to heal. I was sore all over, but I repeatedly thanked God for His protection of my life.

Beyond the Stars

Wilbur Hochstetler

*He brought me up also out of an horrible pit, out
of the miry clay, and set my feet upon a rock, and
established my goings (Psalm 40:2).*

It's 5:30 ALREADY, I TOLD MYSELF AFTER A QUICK GLANCE AT THE CLOCK.
I grabbed my coat and headed out the door of the shop for home.
Joann would have supper ready soon.

The early April sun was fast making its descent after a gorgeous day.
The stubborn snow piles still lying in the ditches were giving way to the
sun's warmth. God had been good to me for many years now, drawing
me to Himself and healing a past I often wished to forget. I shivered
as I headed toward the house, feeling the temperatures plunging again.

I paused to watch a log truck roar past, slowing down to turn into
our mill yard. *Another load coming in,* I thought. Tomorrow would be
a full day again.

I had begun working here 15 years ago, in a business owned by my
wife's father and brother. They had taken me on as a partner three years
later. We had grown the business over the years until we now put out
over 3,000 fence posts a day.

I enjoyed the daily interactions with the workers and customers, so
when the two of them moved on to other ventures, another partner
and I had taken the operation on.

I watched now as the log truck came to a halt and the driver hopped
out to begin unloading the small-diameter logs.

Moments later I pushed the front door to the house open and
stepped inside. Joann met me with a smile. "Supper will be ready in
forty-five minutes," she said.

"I'm going to check on the cows," I said. "Are the boys doing their chores?"

"They are," she said, "and Jaylin ran in to tell me his rabbit has little ones."

I grabbed my headlamp and headed for the barn, where I found the boys feeding their rabbits.

"Dad! Flopsy had six babies," eight-year-old Jaylin announced, hardly able to contain his excitement. I gazed down at the pile of fur. New births on the farm were always exciting events, even if they were only rabbits.

"My rabbit is having her babies tonight or tomorrow," Jeffery declared, joining us at Flopsy's box.

"That's great," I told him, turning my attention back to Jaylin. "How do you know how many are in there? All I see is fuzzy white fur."

"Look," he said, taking up a stick. "You don't want to touch them the first couple of weeks. You might make the mother reject them." He prodded in the fur, revealing the squirming pink bodies.

I smiled. "The rabbits might not be the only ones who have babies. I think Queeny's about ready to deliver too."

"We might have a baby calf?" Jeffery exclaimed. "May I go with you to see them?"

"Better not," I cautioned. "Cows can get aggressive when they have a newborn."

Disappointment filled Jeffery's face. With that I left the boys to finish their other chores and found my cattle prod. I always took the white fiberglass stick with me when checking on cows. The beef cows were generally docile, but when they have newborns they could turn protective.

I reached the corner of the field where Queeny lay. I couldn't see if there was a calf beside her. I moved closer and Queeny stood to her feet.

"Yep," I said out loud, "she's got a calf." The little thing was as black as its mother.

Queeny mooed nervously and began to lick her calf. I was 20 feet away or so, and she eyed me, blowing through her nose. I could tell she didn't like my presence in the least.

"Hey, Queeny," I spoke softly. "You've got a nice calf there. I'd like to take a look at it."

I watched for any signs of aggression. If she lowered her head or took a step toward me, I was out of there. So far she just glared at me. I paused and assessed the situation, all while continuing to speak gently to her. She even seemed to calm down a bit.

I took another couple of steps to test her, always keeping the calf between us. I knew she would either begin to move away with the calf or put herself between the calf and me. And then I would be leaving.

Thankfully she turned and mooed for the calf to follow. I moved on up. Queeny had done a good job of drying it. I lifted the calf's tail to discover it was a bull. The calf leaped into the air, running to its mother. Queeny mooed softly, washing it again with her rough tongue.

It always amazes me how agile a newborn calf can be so soon after birth. I could tell this one had definitely been on its feet before I arrived. But had it sucked? Without nourishment it would not survive the cold night. And if a calf didn't get that milk within the first six hours its chance for survival became slim.

I took a guess that the calf must be three hours old, and it kept bumping the side of Queeny's flank looking in vain for nourishment.

I moved closer. Maybe Queeny would allow me to help the calf, but no, she took off, pacing away from me. The calf trotted along behind her.

Frustration raced through me. Queeny stopped some ten yards from me and turned her attention to her calf again. By now the darkness was falling fast, and I turned on my headlamp. It seemed the sun had slipped behind a wall. There was little lingering daylight as there had been during the summer months.

I approached Queeny again. The calf was still bumping around trying to find the source of nourishment. I kept speaking words of encouragement. Finally, I couldn't stand it any longer. I would have to get Queeny and the calf into the corral and show the calf where to get the milk. I had done this before, and it was never an easy task. Usually any attempts to get the mother inside turned her into a raging monster.

"Lord God," I prayed, "You made the cow and the calf. Only You can make that calf suck without my intervention. Please, if it is Your will, show the calf where to find the milk."

I let out a long breath as my frustration melted away. In its place came a calmness. I turned my headlamp on the calf and adjusted it to see better. Sure enough, the calf was now sucking. Queeny was reaching back and licking the best she could. She appeared as relieved as I was.

Looking up into the stars I said, "Thank You, Lord. You care about us—even our little problems."

With one last glance at the twinkling lights above me, I headed back toward the barn. My thoughts went back to a time when I wouldn't have sought God's help. In those days I even wondered whether God existed. Yet it was on an evening like this that God had reached me.

Up until my early teens, my Amish experience had been typical. Growing up and enjoying the community. When I was 14, my parents left to join a more liberal church. They called it a spirit-led and spirit-filled group. I joined in willingly, thinking we were on to something good.

As time went on we laid Scripture aside and depended heavily on spiritual revelations for guidance. Confusion reigned as revelations were given to our leader. He even had a revelation that only he was qualified to read the Bible. Any member caught reading the Scriptures was sharply reprimanded.

Sinful practices were now revealed as acceptable to God. And since our leader's wife had died, my brother and I moved in with him—all by "spirit revelation."

I was to endure a great despondency in that living arrangement. And one evening I went outside feeling especially low. I couldn't stand the man who was our leader anymore. I hated what he was doing to me. I felt trapped. Defiled. But this was supposedly God's will.

I stared into the dark night, longing for peace. The sky was full of twinkling stars that evening.

"My life is so messed up," I muttered. My stomach lurched at the thought of what our leader would ask of me later in the night. I hated him. Yet I couldn't sort out my angry feelings. One moment I was angry at him; the next I was angry at God.

On sudden impulse I cried out to the heavens, "If there is a God who loves me, show me!"

Instantly a meteor blazed across the sky.

Was this real or a coincidence? I wondered. I had prayed a desperate prayer, but I hadn't expected an answer.

I must make sure, I told myself. Slowly I lifted my face, and whispered the same prayer, "If there is a God that loves me, show me!"

The second meteorite seemed to take the words right out of my mouth.

I wondered in amazement. Did God really love me? My heart pounded against my ribs, but I had to know. I prayed again, and there was a third meteorite. This time the meteorite exploded in the midst of the twinkling stars, forever impressing in my heart the love of God.

I believed that night, and the road back wasn't easy. But God helped me.

So that was the background of my prayer the night of the calf's birth. And now, at peace, I entered the barn to finish my chores and join my family for supper.

Yes, I mused, God does truly bless those who believe on Him, and He gives them a peace that surpasses understanding.

The Beginning of My Journey

Miriam Schwartz

*He maketh me to lie down in green pastures: he
leadeth me beside the still waters (Psalm 23:2).*

I GROANED WEAKLY, FLOPPING ON OUR HOMEMADE LOUNGE. "MOM, I don't feel well!"

So began 2005 and my journey toward a serious illness. We came from the Amish church in Berne, Indiana, whose *Ordnung* forbade such things as stuffed couches and recliners. So my resting place that day was our lounge—as we called it. It was really a foldout English bed with a headboard. We folded it up and made a homemade cushion for it, and that was our lounge.

We lived one day at a time, committing each day to God, not knowing what He had in store for us in the months ahead. But we trusted Him.

I was nine years old that year, and still in school. We thought my getting sick on the first of March must be due to one of those unwelcome flu bugs going around. But it was not so.

While I lay on the lounge my thoughts started running. *I'm not sick,* I told myself. *I feel perfectly okay. So why am I lying here? I should get up and join my family who are having a lively time at the supper table. But, oh…I feel so weak!*

I realized how weak I actually was while trying to get up. So I flopped back down and softly cried myself to sleep. Upon my awakening, Mom offered me a sandwich, but thinking about food made me want to throw up. But both of my parents told me I had to eat a little something to keep my strength up. Gagging, I got two bites of my usually favorite sandwich (peanut butter and strawberry jam) down my throat before giving up.

From then on, every day I got worse and eventually Mom began to get alarmed. "What do you suppose is wrong with her?" she asked Dad one evening.

"Oh, it's probably just the flu that's going around," Dad answered casually.

I awoke the next morning to a supposed fresh start. I felt quite a bit better and crept downstairs to find everyone except little Melvin Jr. ready to eat breakfast. Slipping in beside my younger sister on the bench, I asked my parents why they hadn't woken me.

No one said anything, so I asked, "May I go to school today?"

"Miriam," Dad said sadly, "you don't look well enough to go."

How heartbreaking! And on my way downstairs I had been rejoicing that I felt well enough for school. I had already missed the whole week. What I didn't realize until I heard Dad and Mom talking about me later in the day was that my skin appeared shrunken on my face and I had a bluish tint.

By forenoon, Mom asked me if I'd be able to walk the half mile down the road to Grandpa Wengerd's place. They were Mom's parents, and she needed to give Grandma her bath. Grandma had been an invalid for six years from several stokes that had paralyzed her left side. She also had diabetes and couldn't take care of herself, and was thus dependent on her husband and children.

I agreed, since Grandma was very special to me. Mom's youngest brother, Johnny, had married Marianna Schwartz, and they lived in the big house while Grandpa and Grandma were nestled in the *dawdy haus*.

We set out walking with Mom pulling our flyer wagon. Melvin Jr. at four years old considered himself too big for a wagon ride. So when I, his big sister, climbed on the wagon a quarter mile down the road, Melvin Jr. thought this very funny. He marched along beside Mom, glancing back every so often at me and jumping up and down with glee.

When we arrived, Melvin Jr. soon forgot about me. Grandpa gave him some of his bubblegum—which was Grandpa's usual custom when grandchildren came. I didn't want any, as my jaws felt too stiff to even think of chewing gum.

Mom quickly gave Grandma her bath so we could be on our way

home. I was in extreme distress by then, and very uncomfortable. I didn't know what I wanted. It seemed like I wanted something badly, but couldn't get it.

Mom had one more quick stop at Johnny's house. She had to pass on some news before we could go on home.

My, my, I thought. *Will they ever get done talking?* I could hardly stand anymore. It felt like someone was pulling me down to the ground. Mom must have noticed that I was getting pale and trying to keep my balance, because I was quickly offered a chair. I gratefully sat down and put my head on the table.

Marianna asked Mom, "Have you ever thought of her being diabetic?"

"No," Mom said.

"Then let's check her blood sugar with Grandma's meter," Marianna suggested.

Mom ran over to Grandpa's and returned with the meter. We returned home first before Mom tested my blood sugar. Against my will, I have to admit. I thought the poke of the needle would hurt too much.

Panic seized Mom when she saw that the meter tested over 400. Dropping everything in her tracks, Mom ran all the way back to Grandpa's with the meter to show them. Rushing into the house, white as a sheet, Mom shoved the meter under Grandma's nose.

Staring crookedly at her, Grandma asked, "What's that all about?"

Mom told them, and Grandpa ran to the neighbor's to use the closest phone. Grandpa called Melvin, who drove us Amish people around sometimes, and in what seemed only a few minutes I was at the emergency room of the hospital.

"It's a wonder she isn't in a coma," the emergency staff told my parents. "You can be thankful you brought her in when you did."

I was soon stabilized enough so I could be sent on to the Lutheran Children's hospital, where I stayed for three days. They did a lot of blood tests until I was in tears, wondering when it all would end.

"Du bist okay," Mom would comfort me, repeating often, "you'll be okay." All the while holding me tight. In my pain Mom told me how

Jesus had also suffered pain by going on the cross so we could have eternal life. It was comforting for me to know that Jesus was there with me in my physical and mental pain.

I left the hospital for my new journey in life as a diabetic. The future appeared uncertain, but by trusting in the Lord not to give me more to bear than I was able, I traveled on.

Next March it will be eight years since then, and life has not been without its struggles. Yet I have been blessed beyond words with caring friends and concerned doctors. Thanks to all who have helped me in these areas. And may God, the only True One, be honored and glorified.

The Continuing of My Journey

Miriam Schwartz

*Thou preparest a table before me in the presence
of mine enemies (Psalm 23:5).*

WHY AM I, OF ALL MY SIBLINGS, THE ONE CHOSEN TO HAVE DIABETES? I silently wondered as I prepared to test my blood sugar again.

After having diabetes for several years now, it had grown very monotonous to test my blood sugar four times a day and take shots every time I ate. Often I catch myself thinking that all this extra care takes too much time. But I also can't shirk my duty or I'll get uncomfortably sick.

So I was open to a new option when it was presented to me.

"Have you ever thought about switching to an insulin pump?" asked Alice, my nurse, on a recent checkup at Dr. Lisa's office.

"Well, I can't exactly say that we haven't given it any thought," Dad drawled. "But we've heard of extreme lows someone else experienced when they used a pump for their insulin. This person passed out and they had to call the ambulance."

"Oh, we'll help you with the lows," the nurse told us. "We can adjust the pump accordingly so you have a normal range. And we actually prefer these pumps. They aren't as hard on the body. When you give shots it brings down the blood sugar fast, while the pumps have a more gentle action."

So we accepted the advice and took lessons on how to use the pump. Later, the doctor's office inserted the hose. I was supposed to keep it in for three days to see how I liked the pump. I did like it, and a few weeks later I got the supplies and went through the final instructions. Now I'm on my own. It took a few weeks of further adjustments, but

I'm now taking my shots by punching buttons instead of poking myself four or five times a day.

I have to change my pump sites every three to four days, due to the danger of infection, but I wouldn't want it otherwise. We feel grateful for the connections we made with Dr. Lisa. At first she was too busy to take us, but in desperation Dad told her we had been referred to the office by another Amish family who had been helped.

We feel very grateful to God for overseeing the little details in our life. Dr. Lisa was indeed the doctor I needed.

"How do you feel about your diabetes?" Dr. Lisa once asked me. "Do you feel you can talk to anyone about it?"

I had to admit that I'm very self-conscious and not open about my problem. I worry people will think differently of me if they find out.

"Did you know one of our nurses is diabetic?" Dr. Lisa asked.

"No, I didn't," I said, amazed.

"A lot of people don't know you're diabetic unless you tell them," she said. "You're as normal as anyone else, except you have a bit more responsibility to look after. There's nothing different except your pancreas has stopped working. And it's very important that you talk to someone you can trust about this."

"I talk mostly with my family," I replied, "and sometimes a little with my friends."

I didn't explain to Dr. Lisa that four months ago I had joined a circle letter with three other diabetic girls. This had proved to be another blessing from God as all four of us can identify with one another.

One girl wrote that she had an extreme high and couldn't figure out what was wrong. She changed everything on her pump, including the insulin, and still nothing changed. Her blood sugar just kept creeping up! Finally it hit her that the whole week had been extremely warm, and especially that day. She had been told that insulin is spoiled by humidity and heat. So she quickly changed her insulin again, this time from a vial that hadn't been exposed to the weather, and it helped. What a relief she felt once she found the cure!

Those are a few of the things we learn from each other. We talk about what to watch out for so little events don't turn into big ordeals. But we still can expect bad days like that, though we also have the assurance that the next day we can try again. Hopefully we learn from the lessons given us. We know that God does not give us more than we can bear.

Those Lemon Bars

Delores Schrock

*And let us not be weary in well doing: for in due season
we shall reap, if we faint not (Galatians 6:9).*

IT WAS MIDMORNING ON A DAY IN JANUARY. SNOW WAS FALLING GEN-
tly, adding to the drifts from the snowstorm the night before. I was by
myself in the house. Dad and my brothers were working in the refrig-
eration shop while Mom and my sisters had gone to help with canning.

The clock was striking ten, and I was going over my options for
baking. We needed either cookies or bars to serve with coffee and tea
for the meal after the services the following Sunday. I paged through
the *Walnut Creek Valley Cookbook* and decided I wouldn't be baking
chocolate chip cookies. We were out of chocolate. Another choice I
liked was whoopee pies, but they took too much time, and the last
time I'd attempted whoopee pies, they had been a total flop. So I
searched further and then right before my eyes appeared the perfect
recipe: melting, gooey lemon bars. The recipe looked so easy. Surely
it wouldn't fail me.

My spirits rose and I started humming, "My Jesus I love Thee, I
know Thou art mine."

I set out to gather the baking utensils and ingredients. I selected
a pink mixing bowl and carefully measured the powdered sugar and
flour for the crust. Next, I went to the refrigerator for the two sticks of
butter I'd need.

Oh, no! No butter! I would have to make a trip to the basement.
I raced down the steps, opened the refrigerator we kept down there,
and strained my eyes to see. Yes! There was butter on the top left-hand
corner. I grabbed a pound and dashed upstairs again. I reached into

the cabinet beside the propane gas range to retrieve a saucepan and plopped the butter in. I turned the burner on high and soon I had melted butter.

I poured the butter into the powdered sugar and flour, mixing it in a jiffy. Next, I patted the crust mixture onto a large cookie sheet. But dear me, how could I be so forgetful? The oven wasn't preheated. Quickly I turned the stove knob to 350. I slid the cookie sheet onto the top rack and now I was ready to mix the lemon filling.

I selected another bowl and studied the recipe. I needed four eggs, and of course there were only three in the refrigerator. I was sure from the earlier trip that there were none downstairs, so that meant a trip to the chicken house.

Rushing to the mudroom, I jerked the closet door open and slipped into my boots. Shivering, I opened the door. The cool air swirled around me and as I launched myself toward the chicken house (without my coat!) I promptly sprawled headlong into the snow. Quickly, I gathered myself back up. There was no time to lose. A few more steps and I was at the chicken house, where much to my relief I found four eggs. I hurried back to the house, kicked off my boots, and ran into the kitchen. I was way behind schedule and now breathless.

I began cracking the eggs into the bowl, ending up with the first one on the floor. Grabbing a towel, I wiped it up and continued cracking eggs. This time I got all of them where they belonged. I proceeded to beat the eggs at a high rate of speed, my arm twirling.

Next was the sugar. I reached for the canister and dumped two cups into the bowl. Now I needed lemon juice, and I opened the refrigerator. *Very good!* I thought. We had lemon juice. But wait! I couldn't believe my eyes. I was short two tablespoons to reach my third of a cup. My mind raced. I was sure there wasn't a single ounce of lemon juice on our whole 80-acre farm, but what could I do but check?

Frantically I rummaged through the pantry searching for a familiar green bottle, but no lemon juice could be found anywhere. My only option was to go across the road and ask our neighbor Rosanna for lemon juice.

I headed once more for the washroom, but oh! The crust was in the oven. *It's probably black by now*, I thought. I made haste for the kitchen and jerked open the oven door. What a relief, the crust was perfect. I took it out of the oven and set it on the counter.

Once more I prepared to go out. I put on my old blue denim coat, a royal blue scarf, mud boots, and pigskin gloves. Outside, a gust of wind blew into my face and I pulled the denim coat tighter as I headed up the lane to Rosanna's house. I trudged through the soft snow, reached her house, and knocked on the door. Rosanna greeted me warmly as I told her about my need for lemon juice.

She was happy to help and I handed Rosanna the Tupperware container I had brought along. We chatted pleasantly about Joe's new baby while she measured out the lemon juice. Rosanna handed me the container when she finished, and I thanked her and then started home.

Once home I resumed making the lemon filling. I stood beside the sink and pried at the stubborn lid of the Tupperwear container. There was an awful *whoosh* as the lid popped off and the container fell into the sink, dumping the contents. I couldn't believe my eyes as the lemon juice gurgled down the drain.

I felt all the energy leaving my body and tears were threatening to come. My lemon juice was gone. But I had to finish what I'd started, so there was no choice but to make another trip to Rosanna's place.

I dressed again for the outside and made my way up the lane. Humbly I knocked on the door, and Rosanna opened. Somehow I got the words out. "Um...I was opening the lemon juice and..."

Sympathetically Rosanna told me she'd be more than happy to give me more lemon juice. I mentioned my fears that I might have harmed my planned lemon bars by the delay. She assured me that she thought they would still turn out okay.

I arrived home to carefully open the container and pour the lemon juice in with the eggs and sugar. I then added flour and baking powder. Vigorously I beat everything together and poured the filling on top of the crust. Then I slid the pan in the oven to bake. I set the timer for 30 minutes and plopped exhausted into the nearest chair, totally drained from my hectic morning.

Soon, the *beep beep* came. The 30 minutes were up. I opened the oven door to take out a beautiful pan of lemon bars. I generously dusted the bars with powdered sugar and cut them into squares.

The next Sunday after church my friend Regina told me, "Those lemon bars are the best!"

I smiled. Little did she know the tale of those lemon bars.

My Night Away from Home

Samuel Chupp

And not many days after the younger son gathered all together,
and took his journey into a far country (Luke 15:13).

SCATTERED PATCHES OF DIRTY SNOW DAPPLED THE SIDE OF THE RAIL-
road as I walked between the rails, knowing they led south to the town
of Cadillac, about ten miles away.

I shifted my pack. In it were the supplies I needed for my journey. Some clothes, food, and a little money. There was also a stack of
tourist magazines. The pictures showed mountains, rivers, woodlands,
covered bridges, ranches, vineyards, ski slopes, dog teams...the stuff
of poetry.

I was a young Amish farm boy, with never enough time to explore
these things. And there had been too many restrictions placed on
me. But that was all behind me now. I had ripped off my suspenders moments earlier. They would be a dead giveaway as to my former
identity. My denim overcoat was stuffed in my backpack. I was wear-
ing a tan *English* undercoat Mom had picked up at a secondhand store
with the intentions of using it as a cheap coat liner for me. I had now
put it to better use.

I didn't wish to attract attention. I had chosen my route carefully—
through the bedroom window, into the spruce woods behind the barn,
across about a mile of wilderness area, and down a few miles of back
road surrounded by mostly woods and swamp.

Now I was safely at the railroad tracks. This was a lonely stretch of
rails, and I shivered. The pale warmth of the afternoon sun was fast slipping westward, but the air still had a springlike feel to it. I took a deep
breath, savoring the stirring in my heart. I had decided I would travel a

year or so, taking in work at some of the beautiful ski resorts, orchards, or other fun places listed in my tourist magazines. No more of Dad's scolding, no more restrictions. Only in time would I return.

A familiar song came into my mind, and I began humming softly. "Redeemed how I love to proclaim it; redeemed by the blood of the Lamb…"

The utter hypocrisy of it struck me. I was deliberately ignoring the blood of the Lamb by walking away from my home. But I didn't know any worldly songs to hum. Deep down I knew I was overreacting to my situation at home. Still, I was leaving. I had dreamed of this for years.

Darkness was softening the woods when I caught sight of Cadillac's twinkling lights. I paused for a moment and found a log away from the tracks where I could watch the world without exposing myself. All I could hear was the normal drone of traffic on the adjacent US 131 and an occasional car on Boon Road in front of me.

I started walking again. I would need a place to stay for the night. Maybe the motel on Mitchell Street.

I made my way in that direction, stopping in along the way at a place on Kindal Alley. The name was Topping, which didn't give much of a clue about what went on there. I had wanted to see the place myself for a long time. So I approached the building. The front door was obviously not used, so I went around the back. Yes, there were vehicles in a small parking lot. There was also a well-used door. I squirmed in my shoes, thinking that it was nice that it was dark, and certainly it was nice to slip in the back way.

Right next to the door was an open window. A young fellow, not much older than myself, greeted me. "Let me see your ID," he said.

"ID?" I stammered. "I have a birth certificate." I opened my wallet.

"Birth certificates won't work," the young man said. "It has to be a photo ID."

Dripping disappointment, I cast a lingering look through the window. But there was apparently no way inside. Back on the sidewalk I turned my face south again and started walking.

I arrived at the motel soon enough. I tapped the bell at the check-in window and waited. I tapped again, and from somewhere inside the building footsteps sounded. A lady appeared. "Can I see your ID?" she asked.

Why was everyone asking for my ID? Was there some kind of conspiracy going on?

This time I didn't ask before reaching into my wallet and pulling out my birth certificate. The lady looked at the certificate with mild irritation. "How old are you?"

"Sixteen."

"You have to be eighteen to check in here," she told me.

Gulp! Now where would I go? Apparently I could accomplish nothing until morning. Well…I had my sleeping bag with me. I could curl up under a tree somewhere. I retraced my steps to the railroad. I leaned my pack against the tree and crawled inside the sleeping bag. I awoke frequently to shift positions, but I couldn't stay warm. After several hours of this, I rolled up my sleeping bag and made my way to a nearby Shell gas station. It was still the middle of the night.

The fellow behind the counter looked up when the door opened, greeting me with a friendly "hello." He probably didn't get too many customers at this hour.

"Hello," I replied.

My, it was nice and warm in here. I looked around and saw a rack of magazines and a good selection of snacks and sweets. The young man behind the counter was still eyeing me. He seemed curious and I figured I owed him an explanation.

"I don't really need anything," I explained. "But if it's okay, I might stay in here awhile. I was sleeping outside and I got cold."

"Whereabouts?" he asked.

"Next to the railroad," I said.

"It's February, man! No wonder you got cold."

I figured my cheeks colored a bit at my ridiculous situation, so I came right out and said it. "I used to be Amish. I left home last night."

"What's it like being Amish?" he asked.

I shrugged. "It's okay, but it can get a little boring sometimes. I want to get out and do some traveling."

He seemed happy with that, so I purchased a snack and sat down at one of the tables. My eye was drawn to the magazine rack. "Mind if I look at some of these?" I asked.

"Sure, go ahead." He seemed eager, somehow. There was a trace of a grin on his face as he watched me filling my mind with the suggestive pictures in those magazines. Soon I was back on the street again. It was still dark…and cold.

A car drove by, and then it slowed down and stopped just in front of me. Oops! It had lights on top.

Two officers got out of the car and came toward me. *Keep a businesslike attitude*, I told myself. *That's your only hope.*

"Where are you going?" one of the officers asked.

"Just out for a morning stroll." I desperately hoped I sounded offhanded.

"At four-thirty in the morning?" They glanced at each other knowingly. "How old are you?"

"Almost seventeen," I said.

"Do your parents know you're gone?"

"No," I admitted, and soon found myself escorted to the police car.

"You can put your backpack in there," I was told, and then I received a pat-down.

"We always do this," the officer apologized. "Just to make sure."

"Can I see your ID?" came next.

I meekly handed over my birth certificate, which would give access to my family's information. My travels were over.

Through the haze of my imagination I tried to envision the situation I would face when I returned home. How would I cope? One slight comfort was the woods and wilderness areas around home. At first I would spend as much time out there as possible to avoid the shocked gaze of people everywhere I went. Perhaps I could even arrive at church late and leave immediately afterward. I would skip out on all the gatherings possible. My family wouldn't return to normal for weeks. I would be seen as the boy who ran away. They would wonder why I had suddenly gone wild.

The officer was waiting. Well, there was no way out of this predicament. The first streaks of dawn had already started their work on the eastern rim of the morning sky. I concentrated on the hills, the sky, the fire lanes in the jack pines, and the gravel road beneath the police car on the trip home.

"I'll go to the door with you," one of the officers said when we arrived. He knew 16-year-olds and what they did under pressure. When Mom opened the front door, he excused himself and went on his way.

"We're glad you came back," Mom said. "Would you like some breakfast?"

"No, I had some snacks," I said, still standing at the door. "But I'm tired."

Dad appeared and greeted me. "Good morning. We're glad you're back."

"Let's go inside," Mom said. "Then you can change your pants." She fussed over me, just like a good mom would.

All my siblings were seated around the kitchen table. Dorcas had been crying. Mary was still blowing her nose. She gave me a welcoming look through watery red eyes. Stephen sat looking at his plate, and Jonathan stared at me. Ruby was only ten and didn't know what to do with herself.

I fled upstairs. Back in my room things seemed comfortably normal. There was the bunk bed where Stephen slept last night. Here was the nightstand, the closet, the dresser. I opened the drawer and pulled out a pair of pants—one with suspenders. I turned and looked out the window. Had it been only yesterday that I had climbed out of this room through that window? Everything seemed surreal, my brain dazed with tension.

When I went back downstairs, Dad cleared his throat and said, "I want to say that if there is anything I did to make you want to leave, I'm sorry."

"It's all right," I said.

Like a mother hen, Mom couldn't seem to get finished clucking over me. "Where did you sleep last night?" she asked.

"Under a pine tree in Cadillac," I said.

"I was so concerned about you," Mom continued. "Before we went to bed, we prayed as a family that you would come back. I lay there listening all night long to all the sounds of the night. Every little sound I heard, I thought it might be you returning. Several times I thought I heard you and got up to look out the window. Always it was just something else—the wind, the dog, one of the children upstairs, a vehicle going by…"

Suddenly I saw it—me standing at the door to a den of sin and my family at home praying for me. Me trying to check into to a motel and Mom and Dad kneeling beside their bed praying for me. Me trying to find shelter in the gas station, Mom lying in bed listening for me. Those prayers had come before the throne of God. He had sent two of His angels in police uniforms to put me into a patrol car.

For the first time I also saw something else. The story that Jesus told was about me—a young boy tired of listening to his dad, leaving home, spending his treasure (or trying to anyway), the father listening for his footsteps, watching for his familiar figure, waiting for his return. Always ready to roll out a welcome.

I had been angered at Dad, but I had undoubtedly hurt Mom more deeply than I had Dad. I wasn't ready yet to embrace what I saw, but the tears came anyway. I was nothing but a prodigal son. From any angle I looked at it, the truth stared at me like a wildcat with gleaming eyes. There was no escaping it.

Mom didn't cry much, evidence she had already cried herself out. I didn't say much that morning. What else could I say? But I wouldn't be leaving home again. Not like this.

A Day in My Amish Country School
Rachel Miller

*And they shall teach my people the difference between
the holy and profane, and cause them to discern between
the unclean and the clean (Ezekiel 44:23).*

CHILDREN'S VOICES FILL THE SCHOOLHOUSE AS THE BOYS AND GIRLS sing, "I've got more to go to heaven for than I had yesterday…"

I enjoy hearing my 31 students raise their voices in song each morning, some singing in clear sopranos and tenors and all the rest joining in to create a lovely mixture of praise to our ever-present Lord and Savior.

Bible story hour this morning is an in-depth review of the children of Israel and their 400-year stay in Egypt. The discussion becomes quite involved. Questions like…Why were the Israelites enslaved? How must it have felt to have frogs in your bed and in your food? Why did the Egyptians loathe shepherding? Where were the pharaohs buried?

Pictures and stories about Egypt bring the story to life. Papyrus made from bulrushes help the younger students envision the basket baby Moses was laid in at the edge of the Nile. The fact that the base of each pyramid is as large as the neighboring hayfield awes us all. After a heartfelt prayer thanking God for His many blessings upon us and a plea for protection throughout the day, we recite our Bible memory verses and spend two minutes quietly studying them.

Several of the students are working diligently where the early morning sun bathes them in golden rays through the windows. The pink geranium on the side table also enjoys the sunshine, and the water-filled prism casts a beam of rainbow hues across the ceiling onto the far wall.

A cute floral green sock monkey nestles amid the flower plants and wooden letters spelling out "For This Child We Prayed." The monkey is waiting for Logan to come swing him by the tail once Logan is dismissed from his special education class in the basement. How he loves that monkey—and even punishes him when he thinks he might have hopped off the windowsill!

My attention is drawn to the clock hanging over the bulletin board. Two minutes are not yet past and I gaze at the painting of a bright sunset with majestic mountains and a tranquil lake. On the lake is one lone sailboat and the words *Sailing for Jesus*. I know that in our life we have rivers to cross and mountains to climb. We must always remember that the sunset is coming, but someday at the sunrise we'll see heaven—if we are faithful.

Our globe is turned to India, the land of Hinduism, temples, idols, and masses of people. It is also a land of poverty where we would love to serve the Lord someday by sharing with His children there. How many of my students will catch that vision of helping other people groups—our neighbors across the globe? Will one of them someday join in humanitarian aid work? Will they be willing to sacrifice for the sake of others?

My students love hearing about the 400-year-old house my friends and I painted in Bethlehem, close to the cave where Jesus was born. I also tell them stories about my visit to Egypt and my other work among the poor of the world. They want to know the names of the Iraqi children we cared for at the children's home.

"Could you speak with them?" asks one student.

"No," I told them, "but kindness is the thing you do when you want to say in a special way, 'God loves you and I love you.'"

The two minutes are now past and Javan passes out yesterday's checked papers while hurrying up and down the aisles. At the back of the classroom he brushes past the row of nature and science books we often use for reports. There we identify things like the kind of butterflies we've caught. We find pictures of the rainforest and Antarctica or we recognize the warbler outside our window. The World Book Encyclopedias are often grabbed for quick reference. Just now, Loren strides past and pulls down the M volume, looking for a picture of a mongoose. That's one way my students learn new things.

The daily lesson plan has been written on the dry erase board. With only a brief glance at the schedule, students pull their textbooks, workbooks, and dictionaries from their desks and a quiet rustle prevails. Names and the day's date are written down and lessons are begun.

Each grade takes their turn being called up to the table in front where I teach by demonstration or through diagrams on the dry erase board. I also add verbal expressions on the many varied subjects. We have the mean, mode, and median in math today, plus fractions and measurement skills. In language there are the eight parts of speech and proper punctuation.

I am blessed with industrious students. No one lags behind, but all bend diligently over their lessons. At ten o'clock I quietly announce, "Recess time."

The students quickly rise and row by row disappear into the balmy sunshine and pure country air. It takes only 30 seconds to empty the classroom. Kickball is soon in full swing outside. I roll the ball for each child to kick with a mighty *wham*! When Aden Ray kicks the blue ball, it flies to the right, then left, then up and over; but it always comes back to me at the pitcher's mound where I yell, "Stop." All those not on a safe base are counted out.

Logan, from special ed, makes his first grab of the day and sits on the ball, grinning happily. His teammates laugh and urge him to throw the ball to the pitcher. The runners gleefully race to the next base. How happy Logan is to have a chance to play. Is that not how life is for all of us? There are so many chances to enjoy our work, our play, and each other. Do we grab the ball, sit on it, and rejoice in childish glee? Probably not.

The handbell soon peals from the open door and recess is over. We're summoned back inside the little country schoolhouse where in art class we do freehand drawings of orange, yellow, and green farm fields and falling leaves.

The poem we write down declares,

Golden leaves are fluttering, down toward the ground.
Golden years are passing, we are onward bound.

I wonder where my 31 students are bound in the coming years. Am I directing them toward paths of worldly fame and fortune? Or are they gathering knowledge and wisdom to serve our great Creator in their youth and adult life? Is our time well spent while we study?

They always seem ready to learn more, ready to dig deeper into the wellspring of knowledge available to each young Amish student eager to learn. I pray that they all will be just as willing to find their life's calling under God.

Joe, the Pet Crow

Harvey Yoder

*But I have said unto you, Ye shall inherit their land, and I
will give it unto you to possess it, a land that floweth with
milk and honey: I am the LORD your God, which have
separated you from other people (Leviticus 20:24).*

AS WE WALKED THROUGH THE TIMBERED HILLS OF RURAL OHIO, MY
brother David and I knew our destination. Our home lay nestled on
a hillside overlooking a valley. The woods, creeks, and meadows we
traipsed through were familiar to us. We loved nature and the country
life. The outdoors always beckoned us, and all the plants, animals, and
birds lived in a world we loved to study and explore.

But tonight we gave the evening beauty scant attention as we
walked along, searching for a certain pine tree standing amongst all
the others. A cry of victory soon broke from David's lips. "There it is!
The tree with the crooked branch."

David was good at this. He could find a stone, a gnarly tree, a thorn-
bush, or even a cohosh plant that might house a crow or hummingbird
nest. This time we were looking for a pine tree with a crow's nest in it.

As we approached the tree, we could hear the faint feeding call of
the baby crows.

We had been told that the crow was an intelligent bird and would
make a good pet. It could even be taught to talk, we were told. We
already had dogs, cats, squirrels, and raccoons, but a talking crow
would top them all.

"Now it's time for you to do your duty," David said. "You're more
agile than I am. Shinny up the tree, but be careful!"

Throwing my straw hat on the forest floor and flexing my muscles,

I set off. I enjoyed climbing, but going up as high as this nest would be scary. The red pine was straight and didn't have any limbs at the bottom, but I wrapped my legs and arms around the trunk and slowly inched my way up. When branches became available, my progress was easier.

When I reached the nest, I pushed a needled branch away and peered at the four baby crows snuggling together, waiting for their mama.

Before starting back down I paused for some sightseeing. I could see for miles across beautiful farms dotting the countryside. In the distance I could see my uncle's farm. A closer look revealed them baling hay on the hillside above the barn. In front of me was one of the highest hills in the community, nicknamed Red Hill. The old-timers said the Indians used it as a lookout point. The artifacts, arrowheads, and even a tomahawk that I had found in the adjacent field testified to that fact.

The harsh scolding *caw* of the mama crow circling overhead brought me out of my reverie. Gently I reached in and retrieved one of the babies. I would need both hands free for the descent, so I opened one of my shirt buttons and secured the crow in the bosom of my shirt.

When I arrived at the bottom, David took a look at the bird and said, "My…it sure looks ugly. It only has black fuzz for feathers and an odd-shaped head. Half of it is beak."

I agreed and we began the trek home.

We found a cardboard box and put in a few rags for bedding. This was the crow's nest and was safely stored in the corner of the kitchen. Before taking our seats at the supper table the family all had a peek at this new resident.

The discussion was lively.

"What will we call it?" asked Wyman.

"Joe seems like a fitting name," suggested Esther.

So we called him Joe. Joe, the pet crow.

"I've heard that the tongue of the crow has to be slit in order for it to talk," said David. "Is that true?"

"No, that's a fable," Dad answered. "They can mimic sounds, count, and even laugh without the aid of the surgeon's knife."

"I hope he doesn't carry off my clothespins or pull out plants in the garden," Mom mused.

"Will he carry off my toys?" little Rueben asked fearfully.

We laughed and finally sat down for supper.

For the next several days, we fed Joe bread and dog food soaked in milk and he grew rapidly. When he was hungry he gave his feeding call, spread his wings, and opened his mouth, waiting. When the food was dropped in he gave a funny cry and the food readily slid down the hatch. Other delicacies we fed Joe were small frogs, tadpoles, minnows, and insects.

When Joe had feathered, we took him outside for a few hours to help him adapt to his natural surroundings. Sometimes, if we left him unattended, he would simply disappear and we would become anxious, thinking he'd flown off and left us. We wouldn't take any rest until we found him—usually under a rhubarb leaf or hiding in a pail.

When we thought he was mature enough to stay outside for the night, we left him there. We probably had a tougher time of it than did Joe as we thought about all the nocturnal animals prowling about who could easily make a meal out of our inexperienced pet. In the mornings we dressed and raced outside. As if to assure us that all was well, Joe came swooping down to meet us.

Before Joe learned to forage for his own food, he'd caw from a nearby tree and glide in to land a few yards away. He'd spread his wings and give us his feeding call. Even after he was an adult he liked handouts. Joe would often follow us around hoping for an easy meal.

"Let's take Joe on a walk down to the creek bottoms," I'd suggest on summer evenings.

Joe had caught on by then, and he followed us kids down the narrow dirt road to a small creek at the bottom of the hill.

"Looks like he's showing off his flying abilities," David said as we watched Joe move from branch to branch, swooping and swerving.

Joe soon joined us along the creek bank, getting impatient as he waited for minnows. We'd herd the small fish into the shallow water, catch them with our net, and toss them to Joe. He quickly dined on them.

"I think Joe's had his fill of minnows," Esther suggested. "Let's find multiflora bushes."

Japanese beetles feed on the leaves of the multiflora, and when touched they would let themselves drop to the ground. We'd capture them in our closed hands where they became quite active, putting up a fight and trying to escape through the cracks between our fingers. Joe waited while we'd see how long we could hold the beetles and endure the tickling. When we gave out, we'd throw the beetle on the ground in front of Joe. He'd toss them in the air and swallow them.

"Two more courses to go," Harvey said as he headed for the hayfield.

The luscious green hayfield was infested with tasty crickets. Spying a big one, we'd dash after it. Joe followed on his stout legs, waiting for his meal. Seeing us make the catch, he came and snatched the cricket out of our hands.

"Joe's favorite dish comes last," Esther sang out.

She knew that Joe loved fat, slippery tadpoles. He almost couldn't get his fill. A small farm pond provided these. Joe flew in ahead of us, landed beside the pond, and tilted his head. He peered in the water for what he knew was there. A few sweeps of the net extracted his dessert, and then the tired band of children and their pet crow headed home, where Joe went to his perch in the maple tree and we went in the house.

In the days ahead we learned that crows can be easily tamed, but being clever, they at times become mischievous or a nuisance. Joe always wanted our undivided attention, and when we'd doze off in the yard Joe would take a tuft of David's hair with his powerful black beak. He'd brace himself and tug with all his strength.

David would wake up to flail around. "You rascal, let go of me!"

At other times, Joe would fly in to watch me work in the shop, perching on the workbench. "Looks like you've got mischief hidden under those black feathers," I'd tell him. "Don't you snatch the parts I'm working on and fly off."

Joe hopped closer, observing my work with a clever eye. His black beak pointed toward the object I was working on, his head following every movement.

"Cut it out; I can't afford to lose a part." I batted at Joe, but he bounced right back.

Then it happened. I looked out the window at a passing team of workhorses hitched to a plow. Joe knew that this was his moment, and he snatched a small part from my workbench. But he didn't fly away. He wanted some fun first. I grabbed at Joe but he deftly side-hopped out of my reach. I pursued, but every time I thought I had him, he'd hop out of reach again. After many frustrating minutes of this game, Joe would drop the part and fly up to the rafters where he'd cackle his victory song.

Joe also stole toys from little Rueben. He'd watch his chance, dive in, and snatch a favorite toy. The black thief would then take wing and perch on a nearby limb. Rueben would jump up and, with arms flailing and legs pumping, he'd pursue the thief.

"You can't have my toy!" he'd cry.

Standing under Joe, Rueben coaxed until Joe dropped the toy and peace was restored.

One day David and I told Dad, "We need to teach Joe how to talk. We've tried to teach him to say hello, but all he says is crow talk."

"Well…one of our customers has a Myna bird she's taught to speak. Maybe she can help," Dad suggested.

So the next time the lady came our way she took Joe along home with her, where she had a programmed tape player that repeated the word *hello* at periodic intervals. Three weeks later she brought Joe back.

"He doesn't seem to want to talk your language," she said. "I haven't heard any words yet."

But she was wrong.

"Who was that?" David asked one day with a puzzled look on his face. "That *hello* that came from the treetop. Did you hear it?"

"That must be Joe!" I said in amazement.

We ran over to the tree and sure enough, there was our Joe looking down at us.

So Joe began to greet the people who arrived at our place with his cackling "Hello." They'd stop and peer around, bewilderment written on their faces. Usually someone came to their rescue and told them it was only a crow. Another trick of his was to follow us to school at times, and with him around there were no dull moments.

One Saturday evening my family had completed their usual work and we children were munching on popcorn under the maple tree while Dad and Mom finished the final preparations for church in the morning. Joe swooped in for his portion of popcorn. I sat there taking it all in as the sun slowly dropped behind the west hill. On the opposite side you could see the silhouettes of deer grazing in the field.

These would be among my best memories of country living while growing up, and of Joe, our pet crow.

A Girls' Silo Filling Day

Grace Ann Yoder

*She looketh well to the ways of her household, and
eateth not the bread of idleness (Proverbs 31:27).*

IT WAS A BEAUTIFUL SEPTEMBER MORNING. THE WHOLE COUNTRYSIDE
was bathed in a coat of white frost that was fast disappearing under the
sun's penetrating rays. The colorful tree leaves and grass glistened with
melting frost, and the dripping dew revealed the true noble colors of
the trees. Even the nippy wind was reluctantly giving way to a balmy
breeze that held the promise of a warmer afternoon.

I noticed all this beauty as I stepped out on the porch donned in a
coat, scarf, and gum boots. I inhaled deeply of the fresh morning air,
which both invigorated me and made me thankful to be alive.

Today was silo filling day. Our family had no older brothers and our
community was too small to organize a silo filling crew, so my two sisters and I would make this a girls' silo filing day. But we were up to it.

Lassie, our trusted farm dog, eagerly greeted me with eyes begging
for attention. After a quick pat, she and I walked to the barn where
our Percheron mares, Queen and Doll, were quietly waiting to be harnessed and hitched to the hay wagon. Silo filling was in full swing in
the community, and we were anxious for our day to get started. We
wanted to get it all finished by evening.

As I pitched the harness over Doll's dappled back, one of the tug
chains whipped up and hit my cheek. How that smarted! I gingerly
rubbed it.

Doll, being the more ill-natured, puffed out her side when I fastened her bellyband so it wouldn't be too tight. After pulling and heaving, I finally got it in the proper hole, but not without feeling a bit
disgruntled.

93

"Your disposition matches your Roman nose," I muttered.

Queen, being more gentle, was soon harnessed and paired up with Doll. I hitched them to the forecart and was just ready to drive behind the barn to hook the cart to the hay wagon when the house door opened. My two sisters, Rose and Regina, appeared, ready to join me.

"Do you have your jersey gloves?" Rose called to me.

"No. Please bring a pair along and also the water jug," I answered.

By the time I had everything ready to head out to the field, the two girls were ready to go. They quickly scampered aboard and we were off, bouncing and rattling down the cow path so violently that Rose laughed merrily and joked, "Shake well before using!"

"It's bumpy all right," Regina agreed, "but it's lovely this morning. I'm glad we can be out in the field on such a glorious day. I'd much rather work out here than do the laundry." Regina wrinkled her nose and we all laughed. Rose and I knew how little she enjoyed housework!

"I'm not sure which I'd prefer on a day like this," Rose admitted. Being an avid cleaner, housework held much more charm for her. "It's a good thing we're not all the same," she concluded.

"Whoa," I called out after guiding the horses between the rows of corn sheaves. "Think this'll do?" I asked, wrapping the reins around the forecart bar.

"Should keep us busy for a while," Rose replied as she jumped off and dutifully bent over to pick up a sheaf. "Ugh, they're so wet it makes them heavier than normal."

"They should dry off soon," Regina said, glancing toward the sun while dragging a sheaf to the wagon.

We worked in silence for a while, every so often telling the horses to go forward a ways when we caught up with our stretch of sheaves.

Regina soon broke the silence, "Grace Ann, does the corn stack on the wagon look like the way Dad does it?" She didn't wait for an answer before offering her opinion. "It looks as if it could fall over on the left side."

"I noticed that too," I answered. "It looks like a lopsided teepee." I quickly jumped on the wagon and pushed the offending side until it stood straighter. Dad had taught us to start in the middle and stack the sheaves teepee-style while working toward the outer edges. This usually worked very well, but sometimes we girls had a hard time getting it started properly.

As we picked up sheaf after sheaf, going down one row and up the next, we sang and enjoyed sisterly talks about the Sunday singing the evening before. Slowly the wagon filled up and the water jug nearly emptied. The sun's warm rays were doing a wonderful job of forcing off our thick coats and our scarves tied behind our ears. We rolled up our sleeves as the sun climbed higher. Soon our arms became scratched and rashy and our steps were no longer peppy.

"I'm about exhausted," I finally said, leaning against the wagon to take a breather. "It takes so long to fill up."

Rose and Regina pitched their sheaves on and took a little rest as well.

"I wonder what time it is?" Regina asked.

We glanced at the sun. "It must be around ten-thirty or eleven," Rose guessed. "I don't think we'll even get two loads done before dinner. How nice it would be to have a silo filling crew here. We could be done in short order. Too bad we're not boys with lots of energy," she added almost wistfully.

"I'm as hungry as one, though," I added. "Remember how Mom said she has to cook as if we're boys?"

We chuckled as we returned to our job.

"We'll do our best," Regina replied optimistically. "Actually, I think by the end of this row, the wagon will be full."

Sure enough, 15 minutes later we were on our way to the barn. The harness jingled and jangled as Queen and Doll dug in to carry the heavy load up the hill.

"Good girls," Regina encouraged when they came to the top. Rose and I were barely visible as we sank in the top of the loose corn sheaves.

Regina skillfully guided the horses over to the silo filler, aligning the wagon with the filler. Then she wrapped the reins securely around the forecart bar. We had great respect for this dangerous machine and took all precautions possible.

I crawled off my perch and climbed up on the old trusty Farmall tractor. As I turned the key the tractor sputtered and purred to life. After waiting a couple seconds to ensure it would continue, I slowly pulled the throttle till it was wide open. The silo filler belt picked up speed, spinning and turning until it reached its max. A feeling of thrill and awe swept over me to see this powerful thing in action.

Just then, Dad appeared around the corner of the barn. He checked everything to make sure it was working correctly. With a smile and a wave he left to climb into the silo. Rose and Regina were already throwing the corn sheaves into the filler. The ever-ready knives hungrily ate up sheaf after sheaf, blowing the end results up the filler chute and down into the silo where Dad was busily packing it down.

When the last sheaf was thrown off, Rose jumped down and ran over to stop the tractor. Two of our little brothers, Harry and David, came running out to let us know dinner was ready. What welcome words!

The boys begged for a ride on Queen's and Doll's backs. We quickly unhitched the horses and pitched the boys up, all the while smiling at their delighted squeals. Then we drove Queen and Doll to the barn where they too were watered and fed.

By the time we were finished with the horses, Dad had appeared from the silo. We walked to the house where the aroma of a tasty meal awaited us. After washing up, I sank into my chair as a feeling of deep contentment welled up in me. Ah! This is life on the farm for a girl! A lot of hard work and toil from sunup to sundown, and often much later; but the reward from working with animals and the soil far surpasses any other occupation to me, even though the monetary return is meager. This farm life leaves memories far richer than money could ever buy.

I Ran the Red Light

Levi F. Miller

*Let every soul be subject unto the higher powers. For
there is no power but of God: the powers that
be are ordained of God (Romans 13:1).*

OH, THOSE STOPLIGHTS WHEN ONE IS DRIVING A BUGGY! I LIKE TO DO most of my business in our small town. The bigger towns make me nervous, and not only for safety reasons. Shopping in the big towns seems to take a lot of money. I also believe that spending too much time in a bigger city gives more reason for temptations. One can see and hear more things of the world which aren't good.

Occasionally though, some business needs do require a visit to the big city. So I make the trip a few times each year with my horse and buggy.

On this particular summer day I was traveling alone, having hitched up Teddy, our black driving horse. He was of a more lazy nature, and disliked going the miles to town. He's often tempted to try out many driveways between here and there.

Once in the city, I take advantage of the side streets and can easily bypass the busiest parts of town. I also get around most of the stoplights before getting on Main Street heading for Aldi's grocery and the always busy Walmart shopping center.

What bothers me the most is one very busy intersection between Aldi's and Walmart where there are many red and green lights with arrows pointing left and right. I'm told that if a car comes up to the crossing line, it automatically activates the light system which soon changes the signal to green. A horse stopping on the same line will not do this, and many times a buggy gets sandwiched between the vehicles. So one is always thankful for a patient driving horse.

On this particular day, I had this hard-to-understand intersection on my mind as I neared it. I was surprised as I drove up to find the lights were red, and quite a number of vehicles were lined up on the far side waiting to cross. But the highway to my right and left was clear, with the only approaching vehicles still at a distance. Quickly my mind began to reason. *Here is my chance,* I thought. I well knew the trickiness of the situation once the light turned green and all that traffic started to move.

I urged Teddy on, and we sailed right across that red light at a brisk trot. I took a deep breath of relief. This time had been so very easy, I told myself. But abruptly I heard a shrill siren sound, which quickly became longer, *re-err, re-err,* followed by shorter and snappier ones; seemingly drawing closer behind me. I was now in a bewildered state of mind, glancing out my back buggy window.

Immediately I saw the *flash-flash, flash-flash, flash-flash* of the bright lights of a police car. It was right behind me in full pursuit. My heart sank as I quickly pulled Teddy to the side of the street, and he skidded to a stop on the hard downhill concrete surface.

By now the policeman had veered in immediately behind my buggy. My mind was spurred to fast action. Was I about to receive a ticket from the policeman, taking all my hard-earned cash that I had saved for the shopping centers? Next, more meaningful thoughts passed through my mind, suggesting that a more humble attitude might just save the day.

I didn't have much time for thinking, but I did remember certain things that had been said in one of the Sunday sermons a week or so ago. The minister had admonished the congregation on the importance, power, and far-reaching effect of two little words: *I'm sorry.* He said this was a good way of ending a dispute, or in coping with some misunderstanding with a neighbor or friend. Rather than a lot of excuses and arguments, one just said, "I'm sorry."

In my predicament, the minister's admonishment came alive, and as the policeman stepped up to the side of the buggy I thought at first I was going to meet a not-so-happy law officer. Instead he had a smile on his face, and much to my relief the first words out of his mouth were, "Your horse has good brakes."

He then asked if I realized I had run a red light.

"Yes," I admitted. And I confessed several times that I had been wrong and said, "I'm sorry."

I felt like a child when he informed me, "Green is go, and red is stop."

All of this was happening while many vehicles were passing us. Some of the folks craned their necks to see why this cop had stopped an Amish buggy. Briefly I explained about the tricky crossing. He informed me that he is usually stationed watching this crossing, and today as he sat there he saw me approaching and knew the light was red. He watched in amazement, he said, and held his breath as I crossed right on over against the light.

Yes, he noticed that the highway was completely clear, and he realized that buggies had a hard time getting around here in town.

"But just be careful," he said. "That's the important thing," he continued. "Just be careful. I want you to get home safely." Then he added, "You're the first Amish man I ever stopped."

And with a friendly wave he let me go. I now felt greatly relieved and very humbled at the policeman's politeness and concern. As I continued my shopping I also decided to strive to do better next time in all respects, as far as I can conscientiously obey our government officials.

How to Have Good Neighbors
Mose E. Helmuth

*And the second is like unto it, Thou shalt love thy
neighbour as thyself (Matthew 22:39).*

THERE'S AN OLD SAYING ABOUT NEIGHBORS THAT GOES SOMETHING LIKE this: If you want to *have* a good neighbor, you have to *be* a good neighbor. And as I think back over the years on the neighbors we've had, I do remember that some of them, try as we might, were a bit hard to get along with.

So our recent move to Wisconsin gave us a fresh opportunity to meet more new people and of course new neighbors. We decided after our move here that we'd take time to meet most of our new neighbors in short order. With this in mind we'd take a walk in the evenings, usually with a loaf of bread, pie, or some other tasty dish to give to our non-Amish neighbors. We found most of them receptive to our visit and nice people to talk with. Our home is a little outside of the Amish community, so most of these folks knew very little about the Amish.

One of our neighbors lives a little north of us, less than a quarter of a mile. When we stopped in he acted somewhat surprised, but we had a good visit. We talked about the area, how long he'd lived there, and so on. I asked him if he had good neighbors before we came, referring to the former owners of our property.

He said, "Yes, we got along fine. Never talked to them."

Later, when the opportunity arose, I asked the man who used to live in our house how he got along with the neighbor just north of us.

He said, "I guess he's a good neighbor. I lived there ten years and never talked to him."

After meeting another neighbor just around the corner and striking up a conversation with him, he suddenly said, "You know, I'm just thinking. We've lived here thirty years, but you're the first neighbor who's ever stopped in to meet us."

I guess we were brought up differently. We found it was a good thing to offer our help to our neighbors when in a time of need, be it fixing a fence, running cattle, or just general repairs around the place. We have been greatly rewarded for this effort over the years. As have others, I know. We find it very important to live the biblical teaching of "Loving thy neighbor as thyself."

Sometimes it takes a sacrifice on our part. I remember one rainy spring when it was hard to find enough dry days to put in the crops. Our neighbor, Tom, who was known to have a wild herd of beef cattle, needed help rounding up his calves and loading them for the sale barn. Since it was a nice day, and I had a field all ready to plant in corn, I was a little reluctant to help. But I did it anyway. It took a lot of time and coaxing to get his herd of a hundred or more into the corral. We finally shut the gates on the last ones. I sure was glad because some were really wild. He proceeded to call the sale barn to send out the tractor to load them.

After a while he came out of the house and said he'd changed his mind and decided to turn them loose because they were having a small sale that day. Now that was hard to stomach. I had needed to be on the planter's seat, but instead I had wasted all that time rounding up cattle who were turned loose again. However, I was richly rewarded by having a good neighbor whenever I needed to go somewhere. And in other ways he helped back. When they left the farm some time later it was hard to see them go.

Recently one of our new neighbors stopped in to ask for help with a water pump he said his wife bought him for Christmas. He wondered if I knew how it was put in the ground and how to make it run. I asked a few questions, soon realizing he was unclear on what he actually had. He said his wife thought that the nation was about to run out of money. She thought all the electricity was going to be shut off and people would have to survive on their own. Therefore she bought him a water pump with a handle on it so he would be able to pump water on his own. He asked me how ours worked, how deep it was, and where the water came from. I had to keep from laughing when I realized his wife had purchased him a six-foot water hydrant, thinking that by raising and lowering the short handle he could pump water with it.

But that keeps life interesting. And our plans are to continue trying to be good neighbors so that we will have good neighbors.

They Said *I Do*

Rachel Troyer

*Surely goodness and mercy shall follow me all the days of my life:
and I will dwell in the house of the LORD for ever (Psalm 23:6).*

MEET SAMUEL AND LINDA SWARTZENTRUBER, TWO SPECIAL PEOPLE
who've touched the lives and hearts of all those who knew them and
many who didn't.

When Samuel and Linda first met, they were both in their mid to
late twenties. Samuel moved to our community from Aylmer, Ontario,
in 2007. We learned to know him as a keen mechanic who had a
unique handicap—an allergy to horses that had him walking or biking wherever he went, and in all sorts of weather.

At that time Linda was staying in an apartment at the Elmer Miller
home with her sister Mary Kathryn. The two had lived there since the
death of their mother in 2003. Their mother, also named Mary, had
died from a cancerous brain tumor after a long and exhausting fight.
Linda inherited this predisposition toward brain tumors, although hers
were all benign. They first occurred when she was only 12 and damaged
her optic nerves, which left Linda legally blind.

But was she handicapped? Not Linda! She rallied with the four
senses she had left and worked hard until she was competently per-
forming most of her daily tasks without the benefit of sight. She even
successfully managed a small bakery. Linda did many things with her
hands and fingers that most of us do with our eyes.

Linda had a determined nature and a strong will to succeed, which
stood in her favor on many occasions.

Through a series of unique circumstances, Linda had the opportunity to spend the summer in Tennessee with her aunt's family, Floyd

and Mille Hochstetler. She loved the challenges and joys of their large and adventurous family. It was a growing, stretching, and delightful summer.

When Floyd and Mille were asked to move to a struggling sister settlement for a year to help out, Linda wanted to go with them and it was decided that she could—at least for a few months. So the necessary arrangements were made, and Linda's spirit soared with excitement. She had long dreamed of doing something great for the kingdom of God.

Several weeks before the planned departure, Linda came home to Michigan to see everyone before she left. In that week of last preparations and goodbyes, Linda was approached by a young man who made known his desire to begin a courtship with her. It was none other than Samuel Swartzentruber. Flustered, dazed, and excited as only Linda could be, she accepted his offer, and she left for the trip with plans to continue the relationship at some time in the future.

After only a few weeks in their new home, Linda approached Floyd and Mille with the concern that her brain tumor had recurred. She was having headaches and feeling pressure behind her eyes. They scheduled an MRI and waited to hear the results. It all sounded much too familiar.

Sadly, as Linda suspected, the tumor was back. Arrangements were made, and she was taken to a hospital in Mexico for her fourth brain surgery. Everyone breathed easier when the tumor was successfully removed and tested benign. Linda returned to Michigan to recover from surgery and to begin her formal courtship with Samuel.

Their relationship progressed, and it wasn't long until the two were making wedding plans. But in the midst of the planning, Linda's symptoms returned. Another MRI was done. As we waited for the results, Linda said she felt well enough to go ahead with the wedding as planned. So it was decided to postpone treatment of the suspected tumor until the wedding was past.

On April 14, a week before the wedding was planned, Linda's dad came over one evening with the MRI results. The tumor was indeed there, and growing. Because of its size and aggressive nature, the doctors could not advise a delay at all—not even for the patient's wedding. They said there was a danger of Linda slipping into a coma at any time.

After Samuel and Linda, along with their family and ministry discussed the situation, they decided it would be best if the couple could face surgery as husband and wife. That way Samuel would be free to go along as Linda's caregiver and protector while they were in Mexico. And so the obvious solution was to have an anointing service for Linda the next afternoon and an emergency wedding right after, minus the reception. This conclusion was reached shortly before midnight, and after it was decided, everyone went to get a bit of sleep for the remainder of the night.

The next morning everyone moved into high gear to accomplish as many last-minute things as possible. Samuel's brother was appointed to notify the guests as well as Samuel's immediate family in Canada. The church family prepared the shed and others brought in benches. People dropped their work and rescheduled their day to attend the wedding and give support. Friends who could not be there in person lifted them in prayer.

Perhaps no other bride and groom realized the depth of love and commitment behind the wedding vows as Samuel and Linda did. Certainly *for better or worse, for richer or poorer, in sickness or in health* were not empty words, but a living reality. And *till death do us part* brought tears to the eyes of the congregation.

After the simple ceremony, the congregation sang the familiar hymns that came alive with meaning. Softly and sincerely the melody and harmony blended. Linda had suffered from an intense headache all through her wedding day, but she was upheld and strengthened by the hand of God through the prayers of many.

And it was that Hand and those prayers that continued to sustain the couple as they flew out of the airport at midnight to face a honeymoon of hospital waiting rooms and major operations. But they could face their trial because of their faith in God and their love for each other. In spite of their circumstances, they held in their hearts the joy of the newlywed.

Samuel and Linda spent one year and three months as husband and wife, more in sickness than in health. Linda's brain tumors grew progressively worse in their recurrence rate and aggressive nature. A baby boy was added to their home after months of uncertainty and apprehension due to Linda's condition. Elijah Hob was a healthy miracle baby. Three months after his birth, Linda passed away, and her testimony was still the same: *God is good.* Perhaps one of her favorite hymns says it best: "For I know whate'er befalls me, Jesus doeth all things well."

Our Bean Bin Tipped Over

Betty Gingerich

And who is my neighbour? (Luke 10:29).

FARMING HAS IT CHALLENGES. IN THE FALL OF 2010 WE MET AN UNUSUAL one. We'd been growing organic beans for years. Every year at harvest-time the beans needed a place for storage. We would borrow gravity boxes from our non-Amish neighbors for that purpose. These would stay in the machine shed until the time came to sell them around February or March. However, our shed hardly had enough extra space for all those boxes, so other options were considered.

Our brother-in-law Mahlon Miller owned a large 800-bushel bin, which we purchased. Just what we needed to store organic beans, we thought. The bin was set up in our asphalt yard. A silo stave was placed beneath each of the eight legs on the bin. During the bean thrashing season of 2010 the weather was warm, with temperatures in the 70s. About a week after the bin was filled, my husband, Rudy, noticed that beneath one leg the blacktop had softened and the stave was cracked. He knew that once one of the legs went down there would be a lot of pressure on that side and the bin might eventually tip over. Should he remove some of the beans?

At that moment an old farmer friend, David Allen, drove in. Rudy asked him to take a look at what was going on. David considered the situation and said, "Rudy, that bin will never tip over. There are eight legs and there's no need to worry."

Jon Berthlaw, who lived near the city, was also there that day. He was interested in buying a team of horses and wanted to see how the team worked, so Rudy let him help with the fall plowing that after-noon. Jon stayed for the night with plans to load up and head for home the next morning. Before suppertime Rudy again considered taking some of the beans out of the bin, just to be safe. Still, David Allen's words rang in his ears, "Rudy, that bin will never tip over." Surely David would know, Rudy thought, wise farmer that he was…

The next morning we awoke to the sound of a slow rain falling. Rudy's first thoughts were of the bean bin and he went to the porch door and peered out. When his eyes adjusted to the darkness, he soon recognized his fears had actually come true.

"The bin *did* tip over!" he exclaimed.

Wide awake now, he ran upstairs calling the children and knocking on Jon's door. Rudy asked Jon to use his phone to call Dave McCabe to bring out his semitruck at once. But Dave's semi was full so he couldn't use that. His next call was to Darrel Urban, who also owned a semi. Darrel responded by saying, "Yes, I'll come."

Rudy bounded out the door to meet the sorry sight face-to-face. I dressed and went out as well, feeling I needed to give my husband moral support. The top of the bin was completely off, having been jarred in the fall and from all the pressure of the beans. In all my life I've never seen so many beans. There were beans all over the place, most of them on the blacktop. The ones that had rolled off on the grass or dirt weren't of any account anymore, as they were dirty and wet.

The beans were now swelling from the rain. Something had to be done, and quickly. Rudy fetched tarps from our neighbor, and we covered what we could. Soon he had the team out and the box wagon brought over. One of Jake's boys began scooping beans onto the wagons. Our girls and Aunt Martha helped as well. I decided I wasn't much use in this situation. With more of the neighbors dropping by, I decided to go inside and bake cookies for the men, since there would be no thought of breakfast for Rudy until all the beans had been rescued.

At last Darrel came with his semi and the men began to load beans. Jon, our friend from near the cities, was right there with a shovel, helping along. And then here came Dave McCabe with his tractor, pulling his grain vacuum. What a blessing that grain vacuum was. All the scooping stopped. The auger was pulled to a side and the grain vacuum began doing the work. Like a huge vacuum cleaner it sucked up the beans from the blacktop. The chaff blew from the dust collector and the beans went into the semi. In short order, Dave McCabe and his grain vacuum saved the day. We will never forget his kindness in bringing it over even without anyone asking. He knew his friend needed help and so he came. The other neighbors who showed up to help were also appreciated. What support we had!

The beans were loaded, except for those on the grass, which were estimated at 25 bushels. Now we wondered what we should do with the beans we had saved. The contract was for the beans to be sold in February and here we were just into November. Rudy decided to call the contractor. The guy told him to bring them in. Either he'd pay now and give a dollar a bushel less than the contract price, or we could wait until February for the payment. We decided on the former.

After eating breakfast and loading Jon Berthlow's team, Rudy went with Darrel Urban to deliver the beans. He came home happy. The beans had been quite dry when they were thrashed, so the rain had not hurt them any.

When Grandma heard about all this she said, "So that's what I heard last night!"

At 11:00 she had awakened upon hearing an awful crash, followed by silence. She hadn't known about the worry of the bean bin going over, or she'd have alerted us to the noise.

This fall the bean thrashing time rolled around, and we have another bin set up. We were thankful to find a 1000-bushel bin just four miles away, where an old elevator had sold out. There is a solid cement foundation under it now, and Rudy said, "If this bin goes down, it must have been a tornado went through."

Jon Berthlow and his wife brought their team down one day this fall to help with the bean thrashing. At the dinner table that noon we got to talking about the last time Jon was here when the bin tipped. Jon's wife said we should have heard Jon's story when he came home, how he couldn't believe the support the neighbors showed.

To which Jon had this to say: "I have never had so much fun in my life! Rudy waking me up early in the morning saying, 'Jon, my bean bin tipped over!'"

To which his wife added, "So this fall when Jon said he's going back, I quickly asked, 'Can I go too?'"

So she got a taste of bin thrashing, and a taste of the food Jon had talked about, but thankfully she didn't get a taste of the bin tipping over.

Hosting Church

Sarah Bontrager

*Not forsaking the assembling of ourselves together, as the
manner of some is; but exhorting one another: and so much
the more, as ye see the day approaching (Hebrews 10:25).*

IT WAS A SUNDAY MORNING IN DECEMBER. I WAS SITTING ON THE BACK-
less wooden bench, listening intently as grey-haired Bishop Omer
preached on discerning God's will for our lives. I was seated with the
20 other young women near the front of the room. Around me some
180 people were gathered; the men sitting on one side and the women
on the other.

With the three-hour service halfway finished, I crossed my legs and
sat up straighter. Bishop Omer now picked up the worn leather Bible,
flipped it open, and said, "I want to turn to Matthew 6." He proceeded
to read the familiar high German words.

I knew it was time for me to head for the kitchen and help Mom
prepare lunch, since the hosting family used the second Scripture reading as their guide as to when to begin the final preparations for the
noon meal. So I slipped out of the room with my three younger sisters following me.

Out in the kitchen Mom was already bustling about. Her face was
flushed and curls of hair peeped out of her white head covering.

"Katie, dish out the pickles into plastic bowls," she said to my sister.
Then she turned to Esther and said, "Set the trays on the tables. We'll
need nine tables and four trays on each table. That makes thirty-six—
and also put nine others out for the cookies."

I grabbed the large 16-quart stainless steel bowl of peanut butter
and began to stir.

"This is too thick," I said in a hushed tone, so the church service in the next room wouldn't be disturbed.

I added hot water to the peanut butter and began to stir with slow strokes. This had last been mixed on Thursday, so it was no wonder the mixture had hardened in three days of sitting around.

"Mom, we'll never be ready in time," I heard my sister Lorene whisper. I turned to glance at Mom standing in front of the cookstove, tending the two 20-quart stockpots on the front burners. She looked worried.

"What's wrong?" I asked.

"The brine's not cooking yet," Mom said, "and it's eleven already. The noodles should be let set to soften at least an hour. What should we do?"

"I don't know," I mumbled. I lifted a lid from one of the big stockpots and peered into the good-smelling kettle of chicken broth made with browned butter and seasonings. I stuck in my finger to test the temperature.

"It's warm," I said. "It'll be boiling before long."

· "But it still won't be ready by lunchtime," Lorene said with an exasperated wave of her hands.

"I'll be so embarrassed," Mom sighed. "I guess I should have stayed with the traditional meat and cheese we eat with the peanut butter, pickles, and bread."

"But this will be ready," I assured her. "Just wait another five minutes. We'll add the noodles, cooking brine or not. They'll get soft in time."

"Well, we'll know next time to start heating this earlier," Mom said. "Let's prepare the rest of the lunch while the brine heats up."

I went back to dishing out peanut butter into small bowls. Lorene put butter on paper plates. Katie dipped out the last garlic dill pickles from the large bowl and Esther set out the cookies our four neighbor ladies had each brought.

Mom stood by the stove, now tapping her foot, obviously still nervous about the noodles. "Girls!" she finally blurted out. "I think I'll dump the noodles in now, even if it's not quite boiling. I can't wait any longer."

"Good idea," I encouraged her.

At that moment, Mary, one of the married church sisters, entered the kitchen and asked, "Do you need help with anything?"

"Am I glad to see you," Mom said. "I need advice. This broth took so long to get hot that I put in all the noodles even though it wasn't boiling yet."

"I'm sure they will be fine," Mary hastened to say. "Bishop Omer just sat down from preaching and the other ministers still have to give their testimonies. That'll be another twenty minutes before the service is over."

"I feel so encouraged." Lorene let out a long breath.

"So do I," I agreed.

"I just hope the noodles won't be mushy," Mary added.

"I don't think that will happen," Mom said, but her eyes were big. "I'll turn the burner off right now. And thanks for the advice."

"You're welcome," Mary said, and left to take in the rest of the service.

"This kind of thing often happens to us," Lorene muttered. "But I guess we can learn from our mistakes."

"Okay, girls," Mom said. "What's left for us to do yet?"

"We have all the trays filled," I said. "Should we wash the dishes?"

Mom nodded and soon we had the big bowls, ladles, and scrapers. washed and dried so that they sparkled clean again. As we worked, the congregation had begun to sing the parting song. The slow rise and fall of the tune was soothing music to our ruffled minds. We began to relax and feel happy again.

The double doors to the big room now opened as the women filed into the cloakroom and kitchen. The men were soon busy setting up tables. They did this by putting two benches together with a pair of wooden legs at both ends. The women unrolled the red and white checkered vinyl tablecloths on the 12-foot tables. We young girls set out the water glasses, food trays, bread, and silverware on all nine tables. And last of all we set the soup bowls at each place setting.

"You can go sit down to eat," Mom went around telling the ladies, while at the same time Dad seated the men. Out in the kitchen we girls ladled hot noodles into china serving bowls. After the prayer at the tables, we served the noodles steaming hot, with two bowls to each table. The noodles sure smelled delicious.

I was kept busy filling coffeepots while Lorene refilled the teacups with peppermint tea. Esther and Katie made sure the peanut butter spread, pickle bowls, and water glasses were kept full.

People visited as they ate, which created quite a din with so many talking at once. We soon passed out a cookie tray to each table. What a nice selection of cookies there were: marshmallow brownies, peanut butter bars, and chocolate chip cookies. There was also banana sheet cake. Tea was passed around again now that the cookies had been served. Then Dad told Bishop Omer that everyone had finished eating.

"If we're done eating, let's pray," Bishop Omer shouted above the din. An immediate hush fell over the room as everyone bowed for a silent prayer of thanksgiving.

Following the prayer, I asked Lorene, "Can you help me fill the dishwashing tubs with water?"

"Sure!" she said, and we hurried to the sink. What a bustle of people there were as the women all helped clear the tables and scrape together the leftover food. Within the hour everything was cleaned up and everyone settled down for another hour or so of fellowship before they left for home.

"Thank you for the good lunch!" the women told us as they put on their black shawls and bonnets to leave. "The noodles were a very special treat on such a cold winter day."

"I guess serving noodles turned out okay after all," Mom told us girls when the house was empty. "No one knew the anxious moments we had."

"I think it was rewarding to serve noodles," I agreed. "And now I'm off to visit friends for the afternoon."

I bundled up to join the other girls down at Melvin's place. We would eat popcorn, play games, and visit until it was time for the youth singing that evening back at our place. Lorene soon joined me and together we walked out the door and down the road.

Can We Go to Law?

Levi F. Miller

But I say unto you, That ye resist not evil: but whosoever shall smite thee on thy right cheek, turn to him the other also (Matthew 5:39).

WOULD YOU PLEASE STEP OUTSIDE WITH ME?" MY SON ASKED SOON after we had returned home from the funeral of one of the older bishops in our community. I had noticed his buggy and horse tied to the hitching pole, and wondered what had brought him to our home this close to chore time.

A troubled look was in his eyes, and a strange foreboding passed though me. He found his voice and said, "Six of our cows were stolen today."

"What!" I exclaimed. "Six cows!"

Having only been married a few years, my son and his wife were just getting their start in farming. They had purchased a small farm with an even smaller barn, and they were making mortgage payments on a regular basis from income that came exclusively from milking cows and raising a few hogs, sheep, and chickens.

The cows were of course the most important part, as the milk check paid the bulk of their monthly farm payment.

My son said he had arrived home from the funeral to notice tire tracks leading to the barn door. As it had been a chilly early spring day, the cows had been left in the barn. My son had pushed open the barn door to stare in disbelief at three cows instead of the nine he owned. Six of his best cows were gone!

It was easy to see what had happened. A trailer had backed up to the door and the cows had been herded up the trailer ramp. They were simply gone.

After the first shock at hearing this news, the full impulse of my human nature gripped me. *We must get those cows back!* I thought. *How can payment be made without the milk check? What milk will fill the empty cans tonight?*

Next, the questions arose: *Why would someone want to steal a young farmer's cows? Did he have any known or unknown enemies? What cattle dealer knew of this out-of-the-way farm?*

My son's place has a long driveway and could not be seen from the main road. He told me he had no known enemies, and had very little to do with any cattle dealers, except one local man who had worked with the Amish in the community for many years. My son had been feeding steers for him, and that very day the dealer had picked them up, as had been planned. Few others visited his farm.

So would this dealer have returned later in the day to back up to the barn and load six cows? The man would have known my son and his wife were at the funeral. But this possibility was mind-boggling.

Of course, we shouldn't have been so ready to jump to a conclusion because things aren't always as they appear. But my son had the phone number of the cattle dealer and went to the neighbor's to call, hoping to ask the man some questions. But no one answered the phone. Which we had half-expected, thinking him guilty already.

Our next move was to contact the local auction barns. After contacting the first one, they informed us that our man had not been there, nor had six cows come in. Contacting the next auction barn, they also told us our man hadn't been at the sale, but six cows had come in that fit our description of the lost cows. But here the manager suddenly was on his guard.

"What's up?" he asked.

After we explained our difficult situation he told us, "I believe these might have been your cows we sold today, but our sale barn policy is that we cannot give out information except to the police or other law officers. Please contact them immediately, and we will give them all we know."

Now we were in a more difficult situation. Our belief in nonresistance was severely put to the test.

In the end we contacted the sheriff, who told us he would be out to the farm shortly. By now the evening was dark. I rode home with my son to his farm, both of us heavyhearted. Soon headlights gleamed and probed the darkness as a shiny patrol car entered the driveway. A heavyset, curt law officer stepped from the vehicle. After his preliminary inquiries, we explained the situation. He informed us he could do nothing to help us or even look at the situation unless we signed papers that would allow him or the law enforcement agency to take action, investigate, convict the guilty person, and bring him to court—and also find the whereabouts and value of the stolen cattle from the auction company.

We realized the situation was much more complex than we had first thought. Our home bishop lived close by, so the sheriff allowed me to ride with him to the bishop's home for advice. After talking things over, we agreed to not sign any papers before getting more opinions from community leaders. So the sheriff left the scene.

After a day or two of recollections, a witness came forward who had seen not only the usual cattle dealer's truck and trailer going in our son's driveway, but also the truck and trailer of another cattle hauler. This was a young man, one who had for some time been on the milk hauling route and was acquainted with every driveway and barn among the community. He had lately taken up a job of hauling livestock. He also was always short on money. And this young man knew of the upcoming funeral and had even made inquiries as to who would be in attendance.

With great relief we now discarded the thought of our usual cattle dealer being at fault. We also traveled to the auction barn where the cows had been sold and personally spoke with the sales manager. He repeated his story, "I'd love to tell you where your cows went, but I can't. Just tell the sheriff, and we will gladly work with him."

But the elders of the church had agreed in the meantime that no one would sign any papers to regain stolen property or to prosecute an enemy.

In the meantime the young cattle hauler showed up at an Amish farmer's place and paid his considerable debt. So he must have been both brazen and honest. After that, we never saw the young cattle hauler again. We hope he may have repented of his ways.

We did find out that two Amish men from a neighboring district had been at the auction barn the day my son's cows were stolen and had purchased three cows that matched the descriptions. They sent word to my son that he could buy them back, which he did at a reasonable price. He also bought a few more cows from a local dairy with money loaned to him by his grandfather. The church also helped, which was greatly appreciated. Gradually my son regained what had been lost.

With God's help we tried to make the best choices, and trust we handled the situation in the proper way.

Special Days in My Life

Lori Miller

*And Jesus called a little child unto him, and set
him in the midst of them (Matthew 18:2).*

EVERY YEAR MY AUNTS AND COUSINS COME TOGETHER FOR A DAY OF
playing games and doing fun things together. This one day we went to
my Aunt Joanna's place. She has five children, our cousins.

On our way there we had stopped at the public library and a few
other stores for some shopping. When we arrived, Joanna and her children had set up games for us to play. We lined up in two rows with the
youngest first and the oldest last. The youngest person had to get one
thing out of a bag, put it on, and then quickly pull it off again. The second person had to put on two things and pull them off again. And so
it went, until the team who finished first won the race.

When lunchtime came, the aunts had prepared a delicious meal of
chicken sandwiches, French fries, and drinks. We ate outside under the
trees where there was a nice picnic area with a table and a little playhouse.

After lunch we had a scavenger hunt with two teams. We had to
go find things like a leaf or some other interesting object. We followed
that up with placing tables together and putting bowls on top of the
table with something under them. Then everyone had to name what
was under them. The one with most correct guesses won.

Later we played a game where we hung a blanket between two trees
with a team on each side. We stood in a row and as soon as the blanket was let down, the one in the front of the line had to say the name
of the person facing them. Whoever said the name first won and the
loser had to join the other team.

At the end of the day we played tug-of-war, where even the big
people helped. Later some of us schoolchildren played our own kind

of tug-of-war. Two people stood on a five gallon pail. Then we pulled, and the person left standing on the pail won.

Finally our day drew to a close. We went home loaded with candy and happy memories. Even though this happens only once a year, that doesn't mean we don't get together at other times too. Sometimes we come together for workdays at the homes of different people who need help with a project like cleaning their home or making carpet rugs.

We once went to my Aunt Julia's house to help them get ready for the next Sunday church services. Usually that means cleaning the whole house, plus work outside on the flowerbeds and the lawn.

On another Sunday evening we all got together for a birthday party. It was for my aunt's fiftieth birthday. When we arrived at the place, my aunt wasn't there. This had been planned, as my aunt knew there was going to be a party, but she didn't know the whole family would be there.

When my aunt was due to arrive, we hid behind the building where she couldn't see us. We waited until she was in the yard before we surprised her. That was a lot of fun. And we had plenty to eat afterward. Later, we played outside games with our cousins.

Thanksgiving a year ago was at my grandpa and grandma's home. My cousins who don't live around here were also there. After the Thanksgiving meal we played Dictionary and Catch-a-phrase. All afternoon there were delicious snacks spread on the kitchen table.

We live on a farm, and that day Dad offered to return home to do the chores while we stayed. I appreciated that. As night fell we played Gray Wolf outside, which is also lots of fun.

Another fun day I had was when some of the people from the community got together for a farewell party. We rented a cabin not too far away. It was located beside a pond so we could go swimming and boating. That evening we cooked supper over an open fire. Afterward we played volleyball and sat talking around the campfire. Some people slept in the cabins but most of us slept outside under the stars.

The next morning we cooked our breakfast over the fire again. We eventually had to leave and life began again. I like it when everyone gets together and does their part so we can have a good time.

Outreach

Louie Weaver

But ye, brethren, be not weary in well doing (2 Thessalonians 3:13).

I SLEEPILY WALKED DOWN THE CREAKING STEPS OF OUR OLD FARM-house. It just didn't seem like it was already time to get up. Not this early on a Saturday morning. I felt my way through the darkened kitchen to light the gas lamps.

After washing my face and combing my hair, I checked to see if my little brother Paul was up yet. He wasn't, so I shook him awake. We couldn't sleep in on this brisk fall morning, not with one of the neighbors needing help with the remodel on his house. And Paul would be disappointed if he couldn't go along.

With both of us awake we started getting ready for the day. We ate a simple breakfast of fried eggs and toast, and as we buttoned on our plain black suspenders, I checked the lunch Mom had packed for us the night before.

Our destination was another Amish community some 20 miles away that our church had helped start. Five families from our community had chosen to move there. They were now busy getting their newly purchased property and houses ready for Amish living. All of them had remodeling projects in progress, such as installing gas lights and anything else that goes with moving into a formerly *English* home.

This was a community effort and we had volunteered to help. Even though neither Paul nor I were experienced carpenters, we could still lend our hands. Since 20 miles was too far to drive our faithful horse and buggy, we planned to ride this morning with an Amish neighbor who had hired a driver.

That van soon pulled in our driveway and we grabbed our hats, tools, and lunches and bounded out the door. We found the van nearly filled with other eager workers and the things they had brought along. All of us were from our close-knit community. The 20-minute ride was quiet, save for a few comments as everyone enjoyed the peaceful countryside passing outside the van windows. This early in the morning the land was still wrapped in fog and looked like it was awakening slowly.

We soon arrived and very quickly the sounds of busy workmen filled the air. There would be no idle hands today. The house was old and hadn't been lived in for some time, so considerable work needed to be done before the family could move in. Our main job for the day was knocking out walls to turn several small rooms into a larger dining and living room. I was glad the job didn't require skills from me above the ability to beat down the right walls and haul trash to the dumpster parked outside the house.

As we worked, we chatted above the sound of hammers and saws. All of us were glad for the opportunity to spend time with one another and catch up on community news. Occasional snatches of tunes could be heard as someone raised their voice in joyful song. But for the most part, our efforts focused on the job at hand.

It seemed as if only a moment had passed before lunchtime was announced. Our tools fell silent as we eagerly washed our hands and grabbed our lunches. We sat outside on the grass to soak up the beautiful fall sunshine. After a silent prayer we got busy eating. Our brisk exercise had made me hungrier than I had realized. The sandwich and homemade pie Mom had packed for lunch was the very thing I needed to hush the growling in my stomach. And to our added delight, one of the crew had brought along a tube of trail bologna. This was now generously passed around the circle of men so each could have a taste.

After lunch we relaxed and chatted for a few more minutes before we headed back to work. The job progressed rapidly all afternoon as we dug back into our respective tasks and tried to finish all the work we could before dark.

At the end of the day we piled back into the van and headed for home with tired but satisfied feelings that come from helping someone in need. I was glad I had been a part of something bigger than myself, and that I knew our work made a difference in someone's life.

Pinecraft Excursion

Norman Miller

*To every thing there is a season, and a time to every
purpose under the heaven (Ecclesiastes 3:1).*

It was unusually warm for January in our western New York State community. The temperature that day reached a warm 68 degrees. Not bad, considering that normally at that time of year we'd be floundering through snowdrifts and trying in vain to keep the driveway plowed.

This warm weather was great—except for one thing that weighed on our mind. We had JetBlue tickets stashed in our kitchen drawer ready to whisk my wife, Marlena, and myself along with our two children, Janelle and Jayden, to warm, sunny Florida the very next morning.

Of course as every northerner knows, half the joy of going to Florida is to leave in the dead of winter and get away from the freezing temperatures and the blinding, blowing snow. It may come as a surprise to many, though, that Florida—actually the tiny village of Pinecraft—is the choice winter destination for hundreds, probably thousands of Amish and Mennonite folk from the North.

While my family doesn't make it a habit to vacation in Florida every winter, as many Amish do—especially the older generation—we had an excellent reason for going this year. We wanted to assist in the convalescence of Marlena's father who had just undergone spinal surgery at the world renowned Laser Spine Institute.

Back surgery is always a serious matter, so this weighed on our mind until the report came back that the surgery was a major success. Now that the outcome of the surgery was no longer pressing on our minds, we could look forward to enjoying our stay in Pinecraft to the fullest. The children were really excited—especially at the thought of flying.

On Sunday, the day before we were to leave, we hosted church services at our house, as is common for many Amish. All the families in our district arrived at our house with their horse and buggies, some on bicycles, and others on foot. It was a busy day with so many people in the house from 8:30 in the morning until around 2:00 in the afternoon. So the upcoming reprieve from our hectic schedule and a chance to relax were something we were looking forward to.

Monday morning finally rolled around and it was cold and crisp, way down in the 30s. A much better temperature to head south than 68 degrees. Marlena and I scrambled out of our warm, cozy bed extra early so we could wash all the clothes before leaving and perform whatever other chores needed doing.

After the children were up and breakfast was out of the way we hurried to finish all the last-minute details needing attention. I had to make a final round through the offices and the print shop to make sure the employees were settled in and all was under control.

I returned from my brief trip to the office next door and we hunkered down to wait for our ride to the airport. When he drove up, we all piled in the good neighbor's car and made the 50-minute trip to Buffalo uneventfully.

We picked a super time to fly because there was hardly anybody around. We cruised through security and located our gate, and then that's when, for me, the wonder of our vacation began. We had plenty of time to stroll over to my favorite spot in the Buffalo International Airport—the Villa Italian Kitchen in the food court. They make the most delicious breakfast strombolis I have ever tasted. And Marlena agrees. Though it was only 10:00 in the morning and we already had eaten breakfast, I wondered aloud as casually as I could if maybe Villa's would still be making those breakfast strombolis we so love at this time of the day. I held my breath. My wife looked at me dubiously and with a bit of concern. I knew what she was thinking.

In the weeks leading up to our Pinecraft vacation, I had suggested we could have a meal at Pinecraft's grand Der Dutchman restaurant for every pound I lost prior to the departure date. Unfortunately, the scale seemed to be malfunctioning and it remained unclear how many pounds I actually did lose, if any. So just to be safe I took the high road and assumed an optimistic number.

Now I could see Marlena waver. But I said, "Let's do it. We don't have this chance very often."

So she gave in and, oh, it was delicious! Just as we remembered.

We boarded our flight and several hours later taxied up to our gate in Sarasota's fine little airport. We were heartily welcomed by my Uncle Ezra and Marlene, who graciously came to pick us up. Wending our way through the congested thoroughfares of Sarasota, it seemed implausible to think that a quaint and quiet little Amish community could survive, no, *thrive* in the midst of such a metropolis.

We motored south on busy Beneva Road and swung into a Burger King to execute our first act of convalescence care for Grandpa—bring home supper.

It was then that we knew we were almost there—because we saw them.

"Look," we cried in unison, gazing out the car window like so many tourists. "The Amish!"

There they were, heading down the sidewalk on bicycles, some on two wheels and others on three. Still others were walking and probably even some, like us, were riding in cars.

Quickly grabbing our supper, we headed south again, but for only a half mile. Then we turned onto Hacienda Street, the northernmost street of the fabled, quiet Amish community in Pinecraft, Florida. We coasted to a stop, spilled out of the car, and rushed into Grandpa's house loaded with food, luggage, and plenty of noise.

The next morning, bright and early, Grandpa, Jayden, and I headed off to the bicycle shop barely half a mile away to rent a better pair of bikes for the children. Grandpa cruised around effortlessly and with amazing speed on his three-wheeler that came fully equipped with a battery motor built into the front wheel—a perfect machine for a recuperating back.

With all our wheels in order, we headed south toward downtown Pinecraft. Biking gaily down the road, waving to everybody we met, the reality of Amish city life began to sink in. There were Amish and

Mennonites everywhere. Old, young, and middle-aged, but not many children. They were on foot and on every manner of bicycle imaginable.

We soon arrived at Bahia Vista Street, that unfortunate, noisy, four-lane blemish that divides the quiet community in two. Here we stopped and before we managed to get across, we were accosted by friendly greetings from acquaintances that Grandpa knew well.

I looked around and discovered we were standing outside the door of Vera Overholt, publisher of the widely used *Christian Hymnary* hymnbook. She opened the door and wondered who this group was standing out there visiting. Upon introducing myself, she quickly invited me and my wife in for a pleasant little visit. Vera is a very sweet Mennonite lady. In her 80s, she still manages a thriving little bookstore, hence our acquaintance.

Finally breaking free from the many friendly people we had met at the intersection, we managed to navigate the children safely across the busy street. Nothing seemed to be stirring, so we decided to check out the Pinecraft Park, that place where so many old gentlemen while away most of their waking hours playing shuffleboard. Before we got started, we were greeted by more friendly faces, most notably our good friend Eddie Kline from Ohio. He invited us to stop in at their house on the way over to the park. We did just that.

Arriving at the park some time later, we sent the children over to the playground while we amused ourselves watching the white-haired gentlemen skillfully push pucks around the shuffleboard. Their pace was slow and measured.

I could feel the stress roll off my shoulders as we basked in the beautifully warm sunshine. As the morning passed, more grandpas kept coasting by on their three-wheelers, some feebly, others spryly, many of them chewing on toothpicks, all gladly joining the pleasant banter being exchanged.

Leaning against the fence bordering the shuffleboard court, surrounded by so many elderly, white-bearded, behatted, seniors, I felt one with them. What camaraderie! I had never witnessed such an idyllic social arrangement meant especially for the Plain and retired folk.

Sensing the time slipping away, we reluctantly mounted our bikes and puttered down the road searching for more long-unthought-of acquaintances. We turned the corner and Grandpa pointed about five houses ahead where a pickup was backing up and said, "Look, Norman. Over there is Floyd."

I gasped in astonishment and quickly pedaled over to him and shook the hand of my former neighbor of over 30 years ago. How little difference such a great distance in time seemed to have made. And such is the perpetual experience among the Amish folk in Pinecraft—frequent, unexpected meetings and greetings of acquaintances long forgotten.

Now lest you think that all there is to do in Pinecraft is pedal slowly down the streets and look for people to meet, I can tell you there is more. From our house on Hacienda it was hardly a half mile to one of the grandest places to spend quality time doing what most men do best—eating good food.

Making our way toward the entrance we walked past grandpas and grandmas sitting on rocking chairs on the porch, relaxing after their grand meal inside. Our mood was light and anticipation was high as we opened the door. We gawked around at the huge place. There was an ample-sized foyer and two-story store in the front to absorb the hundreds and thousands of hungry folk that besiege this place every day. Seating a group of only six people was never a problem as they ushered us into the huge dining area where hundreds of others were already hard at it.

The many pleasant aromas that met us convinced us immediately we were where we belonged. My lingering glance at the massive buffet confirmed my menu decision before we even found our table. Grabbing our plates we meandered along the long stretched-out buffet of yummy salads, fresh breads, and too many hot dishes to remember— so many versions of potatoes, greens and gravy, and meats of all kinds. Chicken, pork, tenderloin—it was all there. And the dessert, pies, cake, and ice cream…there was plenty around. What a fine way to celebrate.

Lingering was easy and leaving was hard. But that's Pinecraft! And what can one say but *Aufwiedersehen*.

All's Well That Ends Well

Grace Elaine Yoder

*For he shall give his angels charge over thee, to
keep thee in all thy ways (Psalm 91:11).*

MY BROTHER, JOHN, AND SISTERS, SHARON AND LORANNA, AND I WERE
on our way home in our wagon from an evening fishing at Hicks Lake.
John and Sharon rode up front and Loranna and I were huddled under
the canoe in the back, squatting on the bumping wagon bed. Whenever we moved just a fraction of an inch we bumped our heads against
the underside of the canoe. Through the cracks we could see that the
sun was sinking fast, and we all wanted to get home before the night fell.

To pass the time, Loranna whispered in an eerie voice, "Imagine it's
years ago and we're slaves running away from the slave catchers."

I imagined and could almost hear the galloping feet of the slave
catchers' horses as they came closer and closer. Bravely I whispered
back, "It's fun under here."

"I think we're going about a hundred miles an hour," Loranna
exaggerated.

I peered at the road whizzing by beneath us. It did look and feel as
if we were going fast, but not *that* fast.

Loranna and I jabbered on, so busy having our conversation in
the dark, cramped quarters that we didn't hear the older ones talk in
hushed and frightened tones.

Klink! A piece of metal rod zipped by right beneath my nose. A
loud, peculiar sound rose around us, sending shivers up and down my
back. The horse swerved. The canoe jerked to the side and bumped my
head. Beneath the wagon the road turned from blacktop to gravel as
we gained speed around a curve. Soon the canoe shifted forward as the
horse took off at a gallop down the hill.

"What's happening?" I managed to squeak.

"Everything's all right," Sharon said from up front. By the tone of her voice I could tell that everything *wasn't* all right.

While I worried, I lost my balance under the canoe and bumped into Loranna as we rounded yet another curve at top speed. Finally the gravel gave way to grass as we went across a field. This put enough drag on the wagon to slow it down, and then we came to a stop.

Quivering all over, I stiffly crawled out from under the canoe and staggered to the front of the wagon. There I met John and Sharon and saw what had happened. One of the shafts had broken. This left us with only one holdback on the horse's harness. John had been driving, and he had a hard time stopping the old wagon without a brake. Neither could the horse stop with only one holdback.

So we now quickly unhitched the wagon while speaking gently to the horse the whole time. Once she was loose from the remaining shaft, we shoved the wagon toward a house which lay a short distance from where we had come to a halt. We figured we should ask permission before we left the wagon there, so Sharon and Loranna went to the front door. A dog made a terrible racket, but a lady soon came out and calmed him down.

"Do you care if we park our buggy by your shop?" Sharon asked after telling a short version of our story.

"Of course you may," the lady assured us.

So we left with our horse and trudged off into the night. This part of the adventure didn't last long, though. We soon stopped at another house where a kind old man gave our horse shelter for the night and drove us home in his red Chevy truck. We sank into the seats, which were quite warm and comfortable after the tiresome walk in the dark, chilly night. A few minutes later we were at home.

John offered to pay the man, but he wouldn't hear of it. So we gave him our heartfelt thanks and bid him goodnight. Our parents had been wondering where we had been, and no doubt offered up grateful prayers for our safe return. Dad and one of the boys went to bring home the horse and buggy the following day. They were able to fix the shafts at a welding shop and drove the rig home afterward.

Barn Raising

Harvey D. Yoder

*And whether one member suffer, all the members
suffer with it; or one member be honoured, all the
members rejoice with it (1 Corinthians 12:26).*

IT WAS EARLY IN THE MORNING OF AUGUST 2, 1990, WELL BEFORE THE first crowing of the roosters. Many had already rubbed the sleep from their eyes and were astir, both men and women. The men had done their chores, gathered the necessary carpentry tools, and hitched the horses to the buggies. The women had donned aprons and hustled around the kitchen to put their last-minute touches on the tasty dishes they would serve to the hungry men at noontime. The day of Jacob Miller's barn raising had arrived.

Those who would supervise the work arrived with a heavy step mixed with a tinge of excitement. But everyone was composed and collected as they anticipated the Jacob Miller family's barn being rebuilt. That summer, while the Miller family baled loose straw from the attached shed, the straw had accidentally ignited with a spark. In no time at all the sturdy barn and most of its contents had been consumed.

I was a young lad of 15 that year, and I can remember how quickly the news spread through the community about the Millers' loss. A date was quickly set when all able-bodied men were invited to help raise another barn. When we heard the news, passed along by word of mouth, my dad told my older brother, David, and me that we should plan to help. Both of us were excited about the prospect, and when the wake-up call had come that morning, we had eagerly bounded out of bed.

Dawn broke and the countryside was bathed in fog as we arrived at the Millers' farm. Many men were already there.

All around us the already well-organized barn site bustled with activity. The *clip-clop* of horses' hooves reverberated through the valley as others arrived. It sounded like the congregating of bees around a hive. Altogether there would be 610 people gathered to help. I wondered how many of the people I would know.

I saw that the first-floor foundation had been finished and piles of neatly stacked lumber had been placed in specified areas. This would make for easy access now that the work had begun. The beam frames for the barn were joined with mortise and tenon joints and secured by pounding wooden pegs into the predrilled holes.

Henry Stutzman and Delbert Yoder were the lead carpenters. They soon gave orders to the line of men placed along the finished section of wall framing. I found an empty spot to help raise the first piece. While we waited I nodded good morning to an uncle I had spotted, as well as some of my cousins. Ropes had been secured at intervals along the top beam, both to balance and raise the wall. Spike poles lay in readiness. We would grab those once our arms could no longer reach.

"Up!" directed Henry.

Muscles flexed and the framing creaked as the collection of men moved like a big machine, lifting the whole length of wall section at once.

"Whoa! South end slow down; you're getting ahead," Henry cried. "Keep it at the same level. Pull on the ropes, get the spike poles, and push."

The poles were fitted with a pointed iron at the end, and these were placed against the beam with a few men pushing on each one. Most of the poles were old and had been used in many a barn raising. After today, they'd be stored until another barn raising called for them.

When the section of wall became vertical, the ropes were extended both ways for balance. Sledges and spud bars were used to shove the bottom beams into their proper place.

My grandpa used to relate how at a barn raising in his past, the men had been insufficient in number and the wall became stalled partway up. That day the men had been urged to give it all they had, but the section wouldn't budge. This was a dangerous situation, and if the wall came down there could be fatalities. The supervisor hollered his concern. When this threat was hung over the heads of the men, the adrenaline surged and the frame went up.

Thankfully at this barn raising, we didn't have that problem.

As the work continued, different applications called for different people to fill the job. This fitting of the person to the task was accomplished with little ado. The slender and the more daring usually were the ones who scaled the beams to secure the mortise and tenon joints, put in the braces, and ride the ridge. Others waited until the rafters were secured until they climbed up to place the sheeting. Some men who feared heights stayed on the ground, making themselves available to cut the boards and tin and run errands.

By mid-forenoon the activity peaked. The skeleton was completed and the men were scattered throughout the building. They placed tin on the roof and boards on the sides. There was never a lull of sounds or activities until close to noontime. The tone produced by a barn raising is unique to the ear and can only be described in part: the drone of hundreds of hammers, the whir of chain and skill saws, the clatter of boards, and the mingle of voices all contributing to the effort.

When the lunch call came, the barn was fleshed out and only miscellaneous work was left to be completed. The sounds slowly tapered off as the men left their jobs and began to congregate for the meal. Leather nail pouches were hung on protruding nails or any other adequate hook. Hats were placed on bushes to air out during the lunch hour.

The double tubs the women used with the Maytag washers had been set out on the lawn and filled with warm water. Bars of scented soap and towels were placed nearby as the men filed past to wash up.

When everyone had gathered they bowed their heads in silent prayer and gave thanks for the food the women had prepared. The tasty dishes which graced the tables spoke of their hard work.

To ensure a well-balanced meal, the women from various church districts had come together to determine the menu. A list had been organized and divided amongst themselves. Now the men filed past the tables laden with food and let their stomachs be the guide as to how full their plates should be. The men seated themselves on the backless benches set up under the shade trees, and since it was harvesttime, the discussions were about crop yields and hog and calf prices.

Conversations soon dwindled as the men trickled back to the barn site to complete the few miscellaneous tasks. Where only hours earlier there had been an open area, there now stood an enclosed barn. The 600 men had arrived and worked harmoniously together since the morning hours. The barn now joined the 500-plus barns scattered throughout the Holmes, Wayne, and Coshocton counties of Ohio. All of them had been built through a combination of planning, sweat of the brow, and trusting God to fill in the rest.

Surely the old adage is still true: "Many hands make light work."

The 100-foot by 72-foot barn towered an amazing 150 feet into the sky. Hard work, apprenticeship, and perseverance taught by their forebears is the sum of the quality produced by those callused hands.

Some of the men now cleaned up while the others began to restock the barn with fresh bales of donated hay. Willing farmers had given enough to fill the barn loft again. Wagons hitched to the big Belgian workhorses pulled up with feed for the animals during the coming winter. On Saturday, the neighborhood threshing crew planned to set up on the farm. The straw would be blown into the attached shed and the grain stored in the granary.

A system of brotherhood sharing was used to pay for the costs of the restored barn. Everyone in the community pays into the fund, and when tragedy strikes, three-quarters of the loss is covered. The farmer is responsible for the remaining quarter, but often even that is covered by donations.

This work follows the biblical example of suffering with one another. By pooling resources the full effects of a tragedy are minimized even in this modernized twenty-first century.

My Brush with Danger

Aaron D. Beachy

*The LORD preserveth the simple: I was brought
low, and he helped me (Psalm 116:6).*

THE STEADY *BEEP, BEEP* OF THE ALARM CLOCK STIRRED ME FROM MY
sleep. Pink streaks of sunlight stretched upward from the eastern hori-
zon outside my window. I dressed quickly and knelt beside the bed for
a short morning prayer, thanking God for another beautiful day and a
good night's sleep. I could hear Mom and Dad stirring in the kitchen.

I donned my boots and hat and headed for the barn, where I could
hear the steady *thump, thump* of our dog Queenie's tail banging against
the doorway. I opened the door to greet her with a few warm pats on
the head.

"Good dog," I said. "Want to get the horses?"

She took off for the south pasture, slipping beneath the barnyard
fence in a black streak. I leaned against the board fence and watched
her go with a satisfied smile. This was a decent morning. The fresh air
was heavy with moisture and laden with the promise of spring. I then
went in the barn and opened the outside gate to let in the horses when
they arrived.

I scooped oats into each horse's feedbox and threw hay into the
mangers. I had hopes of getting an early start and disking at least ten
acres today in preparation for seeding the field in alfalfa. It was near the
end of March and soon the best time to plant would be past.

The thunder of approaching hooves in the barnyard brought me
out of my thoughts. One by one the horses filed in and entered their
respective stalls. I tied each one with a rope and halter before heading
inside, where I knew Mom would have breakfast ready.

After a hearty meal of sausage and pancakes, Dad led the family in our morning devotions. Afterward he told me he planned to clean and till the garden today while I worked the fields.

I wondered why the garden couldn't wait. I had so hoped to be in the field by 8:30 at the latest if I had Dad's help with the horses. But he obviously had other plans.

With resolute steps I walked out to the barn by myself and harnessed the big Percherons. I found a torn strap which needed repair, which took until nine o'clock to fix. Everywhere there seemed to be some little detail that delayed me further. Usually I enjoyed my work with the horses, but today's fieldwork seemed destined to go wrong.

Dark and stormy thoughts churned through my mind. I was 20 years old, but I was also the youngest in the family and didn't like to work by myself. Now the bright morning and the chirp of the sparrows in the fresh air did little to cheer me from my increasingly gloomy mind.

I finally hitched two horses to the forecart and pulled the disk out to the plowed field. Once they were fastened to the disk, I discovered that the pin which secured the evener to the main beam was missing. I trotted back to the shop in search of a replacement pin but couldn't find one. Frustration mounted as the minutes slipped by. I thought of the gang-plow down in the bottom where it had been left last fall. Maybe that would have an extra pin?

So I ran to the end of the field and sure enough, there was an extra pin. However, it was a bit short. Should I use it anyway? I held the pin in my hand as red flags flashed in my mind. This could be dangerous if the pin slipped out. But I could search the shop for a longer one at noon, I reasoned. Right now, I had to get started. When I returned to the disk, the horses were lively and prancing impatiently about. So I bridled them and placed them side by side with jockey sticks.

Handling eight horses was quite a challenge, but I got them down the back lane and placed them around the evener with much hollering of, "Whoa! Back, Bill! Back, Ben! Back up!" and other such instructions.

Once they were hitched I stepped on the disk. Without the lines it was almost impossible to keep my balance, but with them in my hands I could. I hollered, "Giddyap!" and we were off.

The eight horses moved along at a brisk pace as the black dirt rolled out from beneath the razor-sharp blades. Usually the jingle of the rings and the smell of the fresh dirt would have been a healing balm to my heart, but this morning they did little to soothe me. I still couldn't understand why Dad didn't see the importance of getting this field ready for seeding.

In my bad frame of mind I checked my watch. It was 10:30. It was then that the *boom* came as the pin broke. The disk stopped momentarily and a mighty tug on the lines sent me sprawling headlong out across the tongue and eveners to land right in front of the deadly sharp blades. I was certain I would never escape alive out of this predicament. Scenes of mangled body parts mixed in with the freshly tilled soil, as well as stories of other boys killed in similar accidents, flashed through my mind.

I felt something bang across my legs, and the next thing I clearly recall was being on my feet and running beside the horses yelling, "Whoa! Whoa!" The horses didn't stop and I fell down in the dirt, stunned. The horses made two large circles before they came to a stop. I gathered my wobbly body together and made my way over to them. I leaned against one of the horses and took off my hat as I gave thanks to God for His protection. I also asked Him for forgiveness for my complaining attitude toward Dad.

I approached the horses and drove them to the end of the field. There I tied them to the fence. I walked up to the shop and after a long search I found a longer pin. With the pin in hand, I hooked things up again and returned to my work.

My leg was sore for the rest of the day, and in the morning my whole side was black and blue. I also discovered a cut in the heel of my right shoe where the disk blades had passed over. I kept this shoe for several years as a memory of the incident. How I wasn't injured worse, I was never able to figure out. It must have been a miracle.

Winter Evening Chores

Ruth M. Bontrager

Blessed be the Lord, who daily loadeth us with benefits,
even the God of our salvation (Psalm 68:19).

IT'S FOUR O'CLOCK!" MOM ANNOUNCED.

I looked over to my sister Elaine and could see she was experiencing the same feelings I was. Chore time in the cold winter weather wasn't always looked forward to, but once at it, we usually enjoyed the fresh air and our time spent outside with the animals.

"Come on, Elaine," I said as I sprinted toward our garage. "Let's get the chores done before we need a flashlight."

I pulled on my coat and scarf and stepped into my big boots. As Elaine appeared, I grabbed the egg pail and then turned on the hot water faucet and filled two bottles for the calves. When they were full, Elaine and I each cradled a bottle under our arm and made for the barn. Outside the wind howled in gusts and caught our skirts in the frigid air.

"Sure is cold tonight!" Elaine exclaimed, and shushed my response with a, "Shh! Hear that?"

I listened and sure enough, there was the distant *clip-clop* of fast-beating hooves. Dad was on his way home and would be here in minutes.

"He's early," I rejoiced. "He'll be able to do his chores tonight."

Dad taught school and often had to spend late hours at the schoolhouse. I knew he had to prepare his schedule for the next day and discuss school matters with his co-teacher, so we often did his chores for him.

We listened to the hoofbeats for a few more moments but had to keep working. The cold was intense. Elaine and I entered the feed room where we poured our bottles of water into a pail. The milk replacer bag stood nearby, and Elaine plopped in two scoops and then glanced around. "Hey, where did our ladle go?" she asked.

"I don't know," I said, peering first into the cracks between the bags. When I saw nothing, I looked behind the horse's oat bin. All this did was produce a scared mouse who scurried for a safer spot. I jumped back, but finally spotted the ladle under the oat bin. After I pulled it out, I held it up triumphantly and set myself to stir the mixture vigorously. So vigorously that I splashed Elaine's face.

I quickly apologized as I knew the unpleasant feeling produced from a similar shower. Elaine wiped her face with her coat sleeve and we poured the warm, white mixture into the bottles. With the nipples on we headed toward the other end of the barn, where the calves had spotted us the moment we came in the barn. By now they had bawled themselves hoarse. We placed the bottles in their mouths and peace and quiet descended on the barn.

This was the fun part. We clung to the bottles and the cute little calves wiggled their tails contentedly as they shoved and pulled at the nipples. It was as if they planned to swallow the foamy milk in two big slurps.

A few minutes later they were done and butted us for more. We yanked the nipples out of their mouths before they could pull the bottles into the pen.

After that chore was finished, I hurried to the shop to get a wheelbarrow of sawdust for the calves' pen while Elaine went to feed our pet rabbit.

Dad had unhitched his horse by now, and he greeted me with a hearty, "Good evening."

"Good to see you home so early," I told him. I set the old rickety, rusty wheelbarrow beside the equally rusty sawdust wagon and scrambled up and inside. With the pick, I hacked away at the frozen sawdust. I sang at the top of my lungs while I worked. It was a good way to keep warm in the cold weather.

At long last the wheelbarrow was full and I made my way back inside to dump the sawdust in the calves' pen.

When I went out the barn door again, I saw Elaine coming from the chicken coop. I hollered, "Are they done?"

"No," she hollered back. "I only gave them feed and gathered the eggs."

"I'll get the water," I told her, and lugged the pail to the chicken coop. On the way over, the water splashed on my skirt and froze completely in the merciless wind. This left the lower part of my skirt stiff, cold, and awkward. I opened the chicken house door and rushed inside. The chickens greeted me in their own loud language and dived out of the way.

After I caught my breath, I picked up the dirty, frozen water bowl and took it outside where I threw it upside down. The ice only broke after I jumped up and down on the bowl. Back inside, I sloshed water in it and stood back to watch as the chickens rushed over. I always found it interesting how chickens tip back their heads and let the water roll down their throats. I often wonder why God made chickens that way. He's so creative, I suppose.

I heard Elaine call from outside, "Ruth! Are you about done?"

"Yes," I answered. "And we still need to carry wood to the garage, but I'm going in to thaw my fingers and toes first."

"Go ahead," Elaine told me. "I'll feed the dogs while you warm up."

I headed for the house where I stood before the old faithful woodstove. The warmth felt wonderful. It soon had me toasty again, and the smell of supper from the kitchen overwhelmed me. I pushed my hunger away and decided I should take a light with me when I went outside again. When I told Mom, she suggested I use the big flashlight we kept in the entrance.

"And hurry," she said. "Supper's almost ready."

I grabbed the heavy flashlight and met Elaine at the woodshed. We hung the light on a bent wire that served as a hook and proceeded to fill the big black sled with wood.

"We have to hurry because supper's almost ready," I said.

"Well, good. I'm hungry," Elaine said, quickening her pace.

After we had stacked the wood high on the sled, I picked up the twine tied to the front to pull and Elaine pushed from behind. I strained with every muscle, bent over, but still it wouldn't budge. I stood to catch my breath. We consulted with each other but decided we didn't want to take off any pieces of wood. So we strained harder this time. The sled gave a sudden jerk and slid over the bump that must have held it fast.

Since I didn't expect such a quick start, I flew forward, landing hard on my face. The twine flew out of my hand and got buried under the sled runners. I lay on the ground for a bit until my face no longer hurt. Elaine hadn't fallen but she still had to gather herself together. She took a deep breath.

I rolled over and stood up. "Okay! Let's do it," I said with renewed energy. So with many tugs and pulls we yanked the twine from underneath the sled runners.

"Now *push!*" I called to Elaine. We bent over double and made it to the garage. In no time we had the pieces in the wood box, but it was only half full. Another load was called for. After we thawed our fingers, we headed out into the cold again. We loaded and unloaded the second sled in much less time and with also less trouble.

"Let's go see if Dad's done with his chores," I suggested.

"Good idea," Elaine agreed.

We found Dad bent over the milk pail, nearly finished milking our only cow.

"Can we help with something?" I asked.

"Well," he said, "you can carry this pail of milk inside. Then I only have to give the horses hay, which won't take long at all."

At the moment from outside the barn we heard Mom call, "Supper's ready."

"We're coming," Elaine and I chorused.

I grabbed the milk pail handle and we stepped out again. Huge, fluffy snowflakes now whirled thickly out of the darkened sky. The winds had died down and peace had settled on the land. Snow squeaked under our boots as we silently made our way to the house. *No one but God could make something so big and wonderful,* I mused.

Once inside, we shook off our snowy clothes and entered the house all red-cheeked. I took in the wonderful smell of supper again, which

Mom and my sister had now laid out—mashed potatoes, gravy, and our favorite meatballs. We took our seats and all eyes went to Dad, who sat at the head of the table with Mom seated beside him. Just to be home with my family and have this delicious supper in front of us was reward enough for all the hard work we had been through. This evening had been another of God's many gifts He sent us to enjoy.

My First Wash Day Alone

Maria Kay Bontrager

Whatsoever thy hand findeth to do, do it
with thy might (Ecclesiastes 9:10).

MARIA, WOULD YOU HELP LENA WITH THE WASH THIS MORNING?"
Mom asked.

"Yes," I said, and I dashed out to the washhouse where I found Lena
already busy separating the clothes into their correct piles.

"Lena, I'd like to do the wash myself this morning," I said.

Lena looked up at me with skepticism. "It's not as easy as you think."

"I know it might be hard, but I'll have to do this by myself sometime," I said confidently.

"Okay…I guess so," Lena said. She left and I approached the washing machine with excitement, singing my loudest. First, I set the hose
into the tub, but when I turned the hot water knob on high, the full
pressure caused the hose to fly wildly into the air, showering everything…including me. I was *not* delighted.

But I told myself this accident had resulted from not being careful enough. My happy song was now forgotten as I turned the hose
on slower this time. When the water behaved, I added a scoop of Tide.
With that done, I rushed out to the shop for the jug of gasoline to fill the
washing machine motor. I did so, and the motor which sat outside
the house started after only a few tries. I rushed back inside to engage
the agitator, only to find that the water in the tub had overflowed.

I shrieked and almost ran inside for help, but I didn't want to admit
defeat. Instead, I sloshed through the inch-deep water and turned the
hose off.

With a sheepish look on my face, I grabbed the broom and swept the water down the drain, which eagerly swallowed up the mess. When I finished with the cleanup, I added a little more Tide. I then pulled the plug and the agitator willingly started, swishing the water and causing the suds to rise. I quickly dumped the first load of clothes in with a sigh of relief.

Then I turned my attention to the rinse tub. This time I put in cold water with two cups of softener and watched the water with sharp eyes. To prevent an accident I stood beside the tub, ready to spring into action and shut off the water when it was full enough.

After four loads of laundry, I changed the water. I thought I was doing pretty good. As each load was finished, I hung the clothes out on the line to dry.

The spring morning was gorgeous! The sun's rays had shone pleasantly since daybreak and a gentle breeze blew from the east. In our yard, little finches, sparrows, blackbirds, larks, and all kinds of spring birds sang cheerfully. Robins hopped all over the lush green grass as they searched for juicy, fat worms. I favored the outdoors and could feel its urgent beckoning.

I could hardly comprehend how good our great God was to give us such a wonderful season to enjoy. I began to joyfully sing praises to God again. I could hardly hold myself down, but I had to go on with the wash.

I glanced at the clock on the wall. I still had three more loads to go! I hurriedly stuffed another towel through the wringer, but something was wrong. I couldn't control my head any longer. Slowly I was being pulled closer and closer to the wringer! In a flash, I realized that one of my head covering strings had become caught in the wringer and in a matter of seconds my head would be there! Such horrible thoughts that flew through my mind!

With shaking hands I tore my covering off, not heeding the pins. I watched with horror as the covering was pulled closer to the smashing rollers. I gathered my scattered senses and switched the rollers to backward. My covering came back out and I rescued it just before it dropped in the swirling water.

What a shock! But I soon recovered my senses. In another half hour I had the last load through. I hung the last black denim pants on the reel wash line and reeled the swinging wash out as far as possible. With that done, I put the brake in place to keep it from rolling on. I went inside and drained and rinsed both tubs. I rinsed the cement floor with the hose and swept it all down the drain.

I rolled the hose up and put the broom neatly in its correct place. Then I glanced around to see if everything was as it should be. Satisfied, I looked at the clock. I was done.

I hurried outside to feel, see, smell, and hear the wonderful spring day. I jogged out to our small family orchard and wearily climbed my favorite tree where I meditated over my hectic morning, my legs dangling over the rough bark of the gnarled apple tree's branch.

I knew one thing: I wasn't very eager to do the wash alone again, but I came to the conclusion that I had learned my lesson the hard way. *Hopefully it will go better next time. Surely it will!* I tried to reassure myself.

"Maria!" my sister Lena called.

I leaped off the branch, and with renewed energy and spirit, I raced over the warm, tickly grass to the house to see what my next job was for the day.

The Day We Missed the Bus

Crist Renno

I was a stranger, and ye took me not in (Matthew 25:43).

My wife, Saloma, and I had married in the fall of 1986 in Newport, New York. Two weeks later we were invited to a wedding at Jake Mast's in Path Valley, Pennsylvania. We left on the Trailways bus and had an uneventful trip until we got to Binghamton, New York, where we had a layover of about a half hour to change buses.

There were different buses leaving and arriving and neither of us understood a word that came over the loudspeaker. In the meantime, I was on the pay phone arranging for a driver to pick us up when we arrived in Path Valley. When I hung up, I went to the counter and asked the ticket agent how soon our bus would leave. His answer came like a thunderbolt.

"That bus left at 2:30. It was announced twice!" he said. The next bus wouldn't leave until 2:30 the next morning. Trailways was quite helpful though. He told us there was a Greyhound station just several blocks away, so we walked over there to find out if any of their buses went to Path Valley sooner than the Trailways bus. The Greyhound people said their bus had also just left. I remembered seeing a bus leave as we walked to the station. How we wished we'd been there a little sooner.

So here we were. You can call it a honeymoon if you like, but we were all alone, stranded in a big, busy city in late afternoon with nowhere to go until early the next morning. We asked if we could just stay there until then and were told that both of the stations closed at 9:00 that night. We would have to stay outside.

As we hung around trying to decide what should be done, a young woman entered the station obviously in great distress, crying hysterically. Our own troubles were momentarily forgotten. Here was somebody who was in greater trouble than we were. She was carrying a baby in her arms and went to a pay phone along the wall. There she struggled to dial while trying to hold the baby at the same time. All the baby did was cry even more. Saloma went over to her and asked if she could hold the baby, and her offer was gladly accepted.

When the woman finished with her call the baby's cries had subsided somewhat. The woman told us her name was Marie. She said that her husband had left her and she had to move from the apartment she had lived in. She then told us about the discarded food she had eaten from the dump, which had resulted in severe abdominal pains—probably food poisoning. She had come to the bus station to call Claudia, a friend from her church, who was now on the way to pick her up.

By and by Claudia arrived at the bus station. After Claudia learned of our predicament she was very sympathetic and offered to take us to her home to stay until our bus was due. We said we thought we would just wait outside until our bus came but Claudia exclaimed, "No! No! Please don't. It's not safe. I'll take you to my home for the night and bring you back." To tell the truth that did sound a lot more appealing than a night spent on the street in a large, strange city.

So Claudia took Marie somewhere and then, true to her word, she came back and got us and took us to her home. Her seven-year-old daughter, Minnie, was so excited, jumping up and down with glee, exclaiming over and over, "Oh, Mom! They look like Quakers—they look exactly like Quakers!"

Claudia apologetically explained that Minnie had learned about Quakers in school. That was why she was so excited.

Claudia's husband, Jim, soon came home from work. She had called him while at the bus station and told him what she had planned for the evening. Jim had no objections to his wife's charity plans. We visited a while. They were a very nice couple and little Minnie chattered all through supper. They fed us peas and hamburgers and showed us where to sleep in a room upstairs. The stairs and floors were lined with a fine carpet. Everything seemed so luxurious and too nice to step on for fear we would spoil it. The bed was nice too, all fluffy and plush, something we were not used to.

Early the next morning Claudia drove us back to the bus station and refused to accept any pay for her efforts. We were at a loss on how to express our gratitude. A plain thank-you seemed much too bare, as this family was like a miracle to us, or at least a godsend.

But we did get to Jacob and Fannie Zook's wedding. They sang the last stanza of the *Lob Lied* as we walked in. We were a little late, but we had arrived by the grace of God and His guardian angels.

Musings from Our Sugarhouse

Levi F. Miller

I will lift up mine eyes unto the hills, from
whence cometh my help? (Psalm 121:1).

AGAIN IT IS MARCH, THE EARLY SPRING OF THE YEAR. OUR WISCONSIN winter seemed long; frozen in its icy and snowy grip. But eventually with warmer temperatures our beautiful snow is leaving, creating damp, foggy days. Still, the birds are arriving with good faith and cheer from their southern stay and the Canada geese are flying low and fast.

As I came down the path into the fog-shrouded valley this morning accompanied by our two farm dogs, I could hear the chirping of a robin and later a cardinal's notes.

Heading for the sugarhouse, I heard a band of crows loudly cawing in the treetops. I noticed the south-facing slopes were now bare while the north-facing slopes were still deep with snow. This kept the little brook alongside my path rushing downhill. The white birches stood out sharply against the now brown hillside, but the pines looked deep and dark in the early morning fog.

The sugarhouse itself stood still and solitary beside the bubbling brook. To the right there stands the small log springhouse. A pipe through the back wall runs water from the brook unceasingly, in all seasons, into a tub which still holds a few jars of last fall's cider.

On the rugged wall hangs a tin cup that has served many a cool drink on a warm summer day. From out of the springhouse runs a gurgling stream singing among the rocks beneath the footbridge leading to the sugarhouse. This stream joins several other springs and small streams as it meanders through our valley pasture, only to disappear into the neighbor's property.

I sit here in the sugarhouse to watch the steam rising from the pan of rolling, boiling sap. I listen to drops of moisture fall from the over-head tree limbs upon the tin roof. I have plenty of time, not only to think, but to ponder. The only other sounds are the hum of the pan and occasional whisper of the wind against the gurgle of the passing brook.

This morning I brought along a few ears of corn to stick on the porch post nails to amuse and excite the nuthatches and the wood-pecker. Frequently, I throw a few more sticks of wood on the fire, but only a few at a time and in a crisscross position so as not to smother the fire and slow the boiling process. The red and gold flames dance and flicker, dimly lighting the interior of the sugarhouse. The glow reflects in the stainless steel of the syrup buckets on the shelf.

After many years of use, the interior of the sugarhouse looks quite rugged and very simple. The rough pine wallboards are smudged and smoky as light falls on the charcoal drawings and sketches on the wall. The hanging marshmallow bag reminds me of last fall's excitement when the teacher and pupils from our parochial school visited the sugarhouse. They came at sorghum cooking time when the hills were decked in gorgeous autumn color.

From the rafters also hang remnants of collected hornet and Balti-more oriole nests along with painted sticks for wiener or marshmallow roasting. Along the back wall are jugs, which remind me of the neigh-borhood boys' summer adventures in our nearby pond.

In the back there is a lean-to porch on which is stacked dry wood. From the rafters hang the remains of a phoebe's summer nest and on the porch sill, a robin's nest. Straight out from the door among the white birches are a row of steel traps. They bring back vivid memories of last winter's trapline.

For years I have thoroughly enjoyed the solitude and relaxed atmo-sphere of our tiny sugar camp. That is, until this spring when a strange feeling of discontent sprang up within me as I realized how crude, simple, quaint, and smudgy our sugarhouse really is!

Only a week ago we attended a niece's wedding in southern Indiana, a location into which we rarely venture, although it did prove extremely interesting. We found them in the very midst of their sugaring season, since the rolling hills of their community proved to have plenty of hard maple trees.

About half a mile down the road from where we were staying lived another niece and her husband. They had built a magnificent sugarhouse; Vermont style, naming it after Wolf Creek, which runs close by.

When I heard a few of my nephews talking about firing up the furnace at 3:30 the next morning I was very interested to see this. However, I must admit that I thought to myself, *These young men will very likely not hear the three thirty alarm clock after an evening at the wedding.*

But I discovered I had greatly underestimated the ambitious nature of these young men. Had they really gotten up? I got up myself to check, dressing quietly so as not to awaken the other occupants of the house at such an unseemly hour.

I stepped out of the front porch door into a moon-bathed Indiana countryside. The night was exceedingly quiet. Not a breeze stirred, and the air was crisp. A three-quarter moon hung behind me over the barn. I gazed across the fields toward the sugar camp, wondering if the steam was rising already.

What I saw held me spellbound. I blinked my sleep-filled eyes and gazed again.

From the huge steam stack arose an awesome column of steam, caught white in the dazzle of moonlight. It reached upward, upward, upward, fading away into the star-filled sky.

After a brisk walk in the direction of the sugarhouse, I opened the door and entered. Inside it was warm and cozy, and the two aforementioned men were diligently at work. The fire roared and the steam hissed in this large, clean, kerosene lantern-lighted building. The gleaming, hooded evaporator was immense. On one side was a tank that caught evaporated water, which was always hot for washing hands, utensils, and so on.

The sap was continuously flowing into the pan from huge overhead tanks on the left side. On the right side stood a thermometer and when the dial reached 200 degrees, it was time to open the faucet from which flowed the syrup. The filter box did a perfect job in removing all crystals, and from there it was bottled or put in barrels for the Vermont markets.

The floors and stainless steel countertops were immaculately clean as this was also the store for "on the farm" customers.

An open shed was built onto one end of the sugarhouse. It was stacked high with seasoned wood all cut to the four-foot lengths the furnace needed. It kept one person quite busy just to keep the intensely hot fire going, flaming white, gold, and blue.

As it turned out, these young men had decided not to go to bed and had fired up at 1:00. By the time I arrived they had already removed approximately 30 gallons of finished syrup. The setup was exceedingly nice, neat, clean, and handy.

Now as I watch the flickering flames in my own furnace, my thoughts return to southern Indiana. I love my quiet valley, my singing brooks. I love the full-bodied flavor of our home-cooked syrup with a hint of smoke or of toasted marshmallow. I love the peace, the solitude.

I think of the saying, "If you are distracted by outward cares, allow yourself a space of quiet, wherein you can add to your knowledge of and learn to curb your restlessness." Come to think of it, maybe we will just stay with our crude, smoky, little sugarhouse down here in the valley. At least for a while yet.

The Wedding
Harvey and Grace Ann Yoder

*Whoso findeth a wife findeth a good thing, and
obtaineth favour of the LORD (Proverbs 18:22).*

NOW THAT'S DONE," I WHISPERED SOFTLY TO MYSELF AS I STOOD BACK
to admire the many long tables neatly draped in white. They were
awaiting our big day when around 460 guests from eight different
states would be served as Harvey and I were married.

My eyes swept to the left side of the haymow where a row of five gas
ovens stood. They gleamed since they'd been recently scrubbed, and
now they awaited hooking up to the propane tank. Harvey would do
that tomorrow. It seemed the list of things to do never ended, but once
Thursday—and the wedding—came, we'd quit, finished or not.

Tuesdays and Thursdays are the traditional wedding days for our
community. Those two days seem to work well for both preparation
and the cleanup afterward; spaced far enough from Sunday to not
interfere with worship services.

Harvey and I had proposed June 15 as our wedding day and presented it to our parents. We had also kept our ears open for other weddings that might be planned for the same date, although such things
are kept under tight wraps.

I now decided to relax a bit, and walked over to the "eck" (the farthest corner of any given room where the bridal party sits with the
bride and her family and witnesses facing one way and the bridegroom
and his witnesses and family facing in the other direction). I perched
on an upside-down five gallon pail and let my thoughts wander back
to the time when Harvey Yoder had entered my life. How surprised
and unworthy I had felt when he had asked for my friendship. He was

six and a half years older than I was, a sincere young man, serious and mature with a very likable personality—a pleasant man to be around.

After a couple of days of praying and seeking my parents' advice, I felt I could begin the relationship with God's blessing.

So it was on a beautiful Thursday evening that Dad asked Harvey to join him on a bike ride. They halted under a good-sized birch tree beside the road. Later, Harvey would tell me that his heart was pounding as Dad started talking about the seriousness of marriage. Dad had said, "We cherish our daughter and think she would be ready to start a relationship with a sensitive boy."

"So it is a yes?" finished Harvey. He was so elated. He had actually passed the test!

This marked the beginning of a beautiful journey as we learned to know each other better. At times, things came up that needed to be worked through, but afterward love's warm rays shone brighter than before.

Next came our engagement. And then the busy months getting ready for the special occasion.

I sighed as I reviewed what a major undertaking it had been to get the haymow ready for the reception. It had been a perfect goat haven during the cold winter months. This was their shelter where they had borne their young and stayed cozy. The free-roaming kids had bounced around on the hay bales like balls of soft fur. Overhead the white king pigeons had cooed and reared their young in shallow hay nests they had built on the stately beams. Now, both the pigeons and the goats had to find another home for a few weeks until the wedding festivities were past.

One evening when the animals were asleep in the barn my adventurous brothers came in and scrambled up the posts. One by one the pigeons were placed in gunny sacks and transported to a pen in the machinery shed.

Hay, twine, and manure in the haymow had to be cleaned out. That job alone took weeks. My brothers had to back the big hay wagon into the mow. They loaded it as high as they dared and took the load out close to the swamp behind the milk barn where they unloaded by hand again. With sheer determination, they pushed through their aching muscles and blistered hands to accomplish their goal.

Then Harvey brought his power washer over and gave everything a thorough washing. Finally, the only vestige of the goats and pigeons was a faint smell.

On this night an increasing anticipation and excitement filled the air. In all this happiness, my thoughts turned to my precious family. I had grown up as the oldest child in a happy, sheltered home. A lump formed in my throat as I remembered how we'd labored together all these years—Dad, Mom, and my six sisters and five brothers, all of us having formed many a fond memory with each other—though my four-month-old brother, Timothy, would never remember me as a sister at home.

I walked over to the big haymow opening and my gaze swept across the fields. There I'd spent many hours with Dad where we had done fieldwork. In the house I had learned the basic work ethics of housework from my mother.

Could I now leave all this for the man I loved? Had ten months been a sufficient time? Had we learned enough about each other to take us through the thorns and roses of married life? These thoughts rushed through my tired brain. Yet I felt confident God had led us this far and with Him we could have a happy home filled with love. My musings were brought to a swift halt when the slender form of cousin Ruth appeared in the barn doorway.

"Oh, so this is where you're hiding," she teased. "I should have known."

I gave Ruth a warm smile. How I had treasured the two weeks Ruth and Grandma Yoder had spent with us. They hailed from Minnesota and had come to assist with the wedding preparations. And help they did!

Grandma had been a stabilizing effect, especially for Mom. Grandma was old and wrinkled but still very agile and the matriarch of the family. I shared Grandma with 70 other cousins, some of whom she had delivered herself.

Grandma seemed to have so much wisdom. She had served as a midwife and delivered many babies, making many friends with her caring and well-liked personality.

Years ago Grandma had taken me upstairs in her house and opened a chest. She had fondly shown me the wedding garments she and Grandpa had worn so many years ago. Now Grandma was a widow and in the dusk of her life. She and Grandpa had seen some troubling times, but her life showed a thankful heart and she still spoke fondly of Grandpa.

If God so willed and we lived that long, would Harvey and I age as gracefully and sweetly as Grandma had? I hoped so.

"What about straightening up the basement while I make sure all the clothes are ready?" I now suggested to Ruth. "By then it'll be suppertime and with more company coming tonight, I'm about ready to quit for the evening."

"Sounds fine to me," Ruth replied.

And so we spent the evening with pleasant company, and the following days up to my wedding passed swiftly, filled with all the last-minute details. People came and went, prepared food, and wrote all the lists for the cooks, table waiters, and helpers. They brought in and set up benches and chairs by the neighbors' big shed where the services were to be held.

And then it was Thursday morning! I awoke with the alarm clock's ring at four o'clock. My younger sister Esther and I were sleeping on a hide-a-bed type couch in the living room. I had washed my hair the evening before and let it hang loose to dry overnight, so I quickly put up my hair, donned my covering, and looked after some things that I wanted to have ready and out on Harvey's buggy to take along "home" that evening.

Home! Everything was happening so fast my emotions couldn't keep up.

After a quick breakfast and a devotional and prayer, everyone scattered to their various duties. The company took charge and washed the dishes. The house was given a last go-over while Mom and I looked after other matters. I went out to the haymow and turned on all the oven knobs and carefully slid in the casseroles. I knew that soon the cook helpers would arrive and take over.

By the time Harvey arrived, the sun had risen and held the promise of a beautiful day. We greeted each other with a "Good morning." His parting words for the evening before had been, "I'll see you tomorrow on our wedding day, Lord willing." The Lord had allowed the day to arrive, and we smiled into each other's eyes.

I hurried upstairs to my room to change into my wedding garments. Gently I slipped into my blue dress. After I had carefully pinned everything together I donned my new white covering and lastly my black shoes and socks. Harvey came in after I was dressed to change his shirt to match my dress. Few words were exchanged, but then it wasn't needful as our hearts felt full.

Before we went downstairs, Harvey suggested we kneel and have a prayer before the services. I gladly complied.

Afterward I grabbed my coat and bonnet and followed Harvey downstairs, where our four witnesses, Wayne, Anna, Joseph, and Esther, waited. I bade Mom a final goodbye and we were off. Two by two, we walked the half mile to where the services would be held. When we arrived, a bench on the front deck long enough to hold all of us was set up, and we sat there to watch the guests arrive.

"You don't have much time to back out now," Harvey teased.

Anna had to stifle a laugh. "Are you afraid she will?"

"No," Harvey answered at once, and I gave him a sweet smile.

Time passed swiftly and we soon found ourselves seated in the "Abrote"—the upstairs room where the 16 ministers who attended the wedding each took a turn giving us a short speech and then wished us a blessed and happy marriage.

We then rejoined the congregation and the first sermon began. The minister followed the traditional pattern of expounding on the story of creation, followed by that of Adam and Eve, the first husband and wife. Stories were also told of Noah and his sons and how they took to themselves wives of the children of God, and of Isaac and Rebekah, and of Jacob and Laban and Jacob's two wives. Also Solomon and his many wives were mentioned and the story of the misfortune this brought upon him and the kingdom of Israel. All these were important points to help guide and lead us into a godly marriage.

Soon Bishop Alvin took his turn to preach and eventually he closed the Bible and a hush fell over the assembly.

"Harvey and Grace," the bishop addressed us, "if you still feel like this is God's will, you may now come forward."

After a slight pause, we walked up to the bishop and he began the sacred questions.

We solemnly promised before God and many witnesses to love, cherish, and care for each other in joys and sorrows, health and sickness, all the days of our life until only death doth us part.

Bishop Alvin took both of our right hands and placed them together in marriage. "You are no longer two but one flesh, husband and wife. You may now take your seats," Alvin concluded.

Now I'm Grace Yoder, no longer a Keim, I thought to myself as we took our seats. It all seemed so profound, so mysterious, but so wonderful.

When the services were over, Harvey's brother Henry had the horse and a small wagon ready. There were three hay bales for seating. The rig waited to usher the bridal party back down the road where the noon meal was being prepared by the appointed cooks and table waiters.

Everyone was soon ushered into the haymow and seated. After a short prayer the cooks dished out bowls of steaming scalloped potatoes, platters of meatloaf garnished with parsley, and dishes of golden, buttery corn. The table waiters quickly took these to their assigned tables lined with waiting guests. Attractively arranged salads were set out in bowls. Each table also had butter and jam and a dinner roll placed by each plate. The meal was rounded out by apple pie, vanilla ice cream, and coffee.

When everyone had their fill, the table waiters swiftly cleaned the tables and a period of singing followed. The songs were ones we had chosen, and included a song Harvey had written himself. This was followed by a short devotional given by my Uncle James.

Before they left for their homes, many of the guests come up to the "eck," greeted us with a handshake, and wished us God's blessings on our marriage.

Nickel Mines Tragedy

Benuel M. Fisher

This is my comfort in my affliction: for thy word
hath quickened me (Psalm 119:50).

THE RURAL VILLAGE OF NICKEL MINES, PENNSYLVANIA, IS A QUIET community of farms and friendly people, both Amish and English. Many Amish farmers in Nickel Mines till the land and work in the fields. They wave to passersby on the road, whether it be one of their own horse-drawn buggies or the well-known feed, cattle, or milk truck drivers.

On this exceptionally nice Monday morning, Amish schoolchildren walked the rural roads through the crisp air on their way to the West Nickel Mine's Amish School. The boys wore homemade shirts and trousers and had on straw hats. The girls were clad in dresses of blue, green, or light brown, with a traditional black apron pinned on. They all toted plastic lunch boxes and chatted merrily as they walked along.

At the schoolhouse, the teacher, Emma Zook, greeted their smiling faces with a "Good morning." The children then left their lunch pails inside and joined the others on the playground for the few remaining minutes before school began.

At 8:00, Emma pulled the long rope that operated the bell on top of the schoolhouse. Everyone was soon at their desk and listening as Emma read a passage from the Bible. They then stood beside their desks and recited the Lord's Prayer. This had been the formal routine of their parents and their grandparents before them, many of whom had once attended public schools where such things were now forbidden.

When everyone had said, "Amen," they lifted their bowed heads and marched single file up to the front of the schoolhouse. There they lined up at the blackboard for the morning hymns. Each child knew his place. The tallest in the back row, the middle-sized next, and the first and second graders in front. They began with "When the Roll Is Called Up Yonder," followed by "Hold to God's Unchanging Hand," and then, finally, "Amazing Grace." The sound filled the schoolhouse as everyone lifted their voices to honor God. When they finished, each child filed back down the aisle to their seats.

There were 31 pupils that morning, in grades one to eight. The five eager and bright-eyed first-graders recited their basic sounds before the first recess. Emma's mother and her two daughters-in-law, Bertha and Annie, had come to visit and stayed through the 15-minute recess at 9:15. After the bell rang again, all the students took their seats and opened their books to study. Shortly afterward, they heard the sound of a vehicle coming slowly down the road, the gravel crunching as a pickup truck backed up to the schoolhouse door.

In walked Mr. Roberts, the local milk truck driver who hauled raw milk from the Amish farms. The children all knew him as a rather shy and not-that-friendly man. Emma went to greet him, and Mr. Roberts asked if anyone had seen a tool he had lost on the road. No one had, but several of the boys promised to help him search during their noon lunch period. They felt no fear for this man who lived a few miles down the road in Georgetown.

Mr. Roberts returned to his truck and Emma continued her lesson. She was interrupted when Mr. Roberts reappeared, this time waving a pistol in his right hand.

"Everyone up to the front of the room," he ordered in a stern voice. "Lie down on the floor, facedown."

Of course they all obeyed, but no one could figure this out. Why would Mr. Roberts act this way?

"Lie down and do as I say and nobody will get hurt," Mr. Roberts ordered again.

Teacher Emma and her three relatives feared what might come next. Moments later, as Mr. Roberts pulled down the window curtains, the four women were able to escape. There was no telephone nearby, so Emma ran across the fields to call 911 at a neighbor's farmhouse.

In the meanwhile, back at the schoolhouse, Mr. Roberts nailed sheets of plywood over the windows. He also began to tie the girls' feet together so they couldn't escape. He finally noticed the absence of Emma and her three relatives and became quite furious. "Someone better go after them, or you will have great trouble," he said, waving his pistol around again. Then he asked all the boys to leave.

When the boys were gone he snapped at little Susie. "Lift up your foot."

"What's he going to do to us?" a little second grader asked in Pennsylvania Dutch.

"Everyone pray real earnestly. God will hear us," an eighth grader admonished.

"What are you girls whispering about?" Mr. Roberts asked.

"We're praying," came the answer.

"Why don't you pray for me?" he said. "I can't pray. I don't believe in God anymore."

Soon after this, he heard vehicles pull up and stop outside. Mr. Roberts also received a phone call from his wife. But despite her pleas, he told her, "I've got to do this."

He ended the call, and the order came from the police standing outside, "Open up and come out!"

The girls hoped Mr. Roberts would obey, but he threatened them instead with his gun.

One of the older girls spoke up. "If you're going to shoot someone, shoot me, but let the little ones live."

But it was to no avail.

Mr. Roberts began to shoot all of the girls at close range. When the police outside heard the shots and the screams of the girls, they broke down the door. But it was too late. They found Mr. Roberts lying on the floor, some ten feet from the line of bloody and limp girls. He had shot himself in the face.

Rescue workers rushed in and began their work. Several of the girls had been shot in the head, while others had suffered wounds in the back, legs, and thighs. One burly policeman was overcome and had to leave the scene. Once outside, he leaned over the school fence and wept.

Helicopters were brought in and the wounded girls were life-flighted to area hospitals. Several were conscious during the whole ordeal. Two sisters, Lena and Mary Miller, who were in critical condition, were separated, one flown to Philadelphia Hospital while the other was sent to Hershey Medical Center. No one on-site made the connection in the rush to give aid. The parents of all the victims began to arrive, and loving volunteer drivers escorted the families to the hospitals.

The parents of the Miller sisters made their way to Philadelphia to find their one daughter there, but she had already passed on into eternity. They waited for 30 minutes for information on where their other daughter had been taken. By the time they were told, that second daughter had also died.

Back at the schoolhouse, the news media had arrived, but the police kept them away out of respect for the grieving families. None of the Amish wanted their pictures flashed all over the world. Could their milkman have done such a thing? But Teacher Emma insisted. The shooter had been no one else.

Mr. Roberts's body was taken to the morgue while parents waited at the hospitals for further news on their daughters. Three more had died for a total of five dead. The Amish community gathered in the homes of those affected and began to make funeral arrangements. Grave-diggers were assigned for the five graves. One would be a double grave for the Miller sisters. Many, many tears were shed. No tragedy had ever touched the hearts of the community like this.

The Amish expressed great sympathy also for Mrs. Roberts and her small children. Several of them traveled to her home and cried with her. She knew her husband had been having some depression problems, Mrs. Roberts told them, but this was beyond anything she could have imagined. She wept on the Amish women's shoulders and expressed her heartfelt regret. It was made clear to Mrs. Roberts that no one blamed her for her husband's actions. The tragedy would be left in the hands of God.

Before dark the shooting was on the news everywhere. Thousands who watched on TV claimed that Mr. Roberts must have been a man of the devil. And no doubt he did a devilish act, but the Amish decided to let God be the judge in that matter. They remembered how an evil spirit sent from God had entered King Saul's heart in the Old Testament, which drove him to seek the life of young David, the anointed of the Lord.

In the days that followed, many people from all denominations shared their sympathy with the bereaved families. Three funerals were held in one day and two the next. The news media stood along the road with their huge cameras set up like clusters of trees in a forest, and the police kept them all at bay the best they could.

In order to express their sincere sympathy, the local police force had mounted police on horseback to escort the first funeral procession. The procession of buggies was two miles long. Mrs. Roberts watched them pass her home and wept uncontrollably.

After the five bodies were buried, Mr. Roberts's funeral was held the following day. Dozens of Amish people attended and shared their deepest condolences. Many tears were also shed that day.

English neighbors attended the funerals of the Amish girls but were unable to understand the sermon, since it was preached in Pennsylvania Dutch. The scriptures in which Jesus spoke of loving our enemies and blessing those who curse us were read in *English*.

Mail began to flow into Nickel Mines, filled with donations and sympathy cards from every state in the Union. Even sympathizers in foreign countries wished to contribute to the families. Many of the donations were delivered by the mail carriers, even though Nickel Mines has no post office. A committee of Amish and *English* people were assigned by the Amish bishops to handle the thousands of letters. The donations were placed in a large box to pay the hospital bills, which were huge even after the hospitals and doctors reduced their rates. Everyone wished to show their sympathy. The amount of funds was kept confidential, but it was made known that the committee was able to pay all the expenses, even the undertakers' bills.

Food was brought into the firehouse for the hundreds of visitors and volunteers, all of whom wished to help where they could. Letters were sorted. Some of them had the names of the bereaved families and were from far-off places like Montana, Maine, Texas, Sweden, Poland, and Australia. Many were simply addressed to *Nickel Mines, Pennsylvania.* Volunteers spent days sorting this mail.

Packages also arrived containing gifts of dolls and books as well as numerous tokens for the wounded girls. The committee also shared many of these donations with Mrs. Roberts. All her husband's funeral expenses were paid and she received hundreds of sympathy letters from the Amish people.

The five survivors were released from hospitals after having undergone surgery. Rosanna King had been shot in the head, which left her in a coma for months. She received therapy and was finally able to return home to live with her parents. Rosanna is still under the constant care of friends and relatives. As of today, she cannot talk or walk, and may be crippled for life. Her mind is fairly sharp, though. Rosanna attends church and the Sunbeam School for special needs children.

The Nickel Mines schoolhouse was razed a week after the shootings. No parents wanted their children to attend a school where the daily memory would be of such a tragic event. A new one-room schoolhouse was built half a mile away and is called the New Hope School.

The heartbroken families have filled their lives with forgiveness and have moved on in their search of a life pleasing to God.

To Market, To Market

Rachel Troyer

But sanctify the Lord God in your hearts: and be ready always
to give an answer to every man that asketh you a reason of the
hope that is in you with meekness and fear (1 Peter 3:15).

AT EASTERN MARKET IN DETROIT ON A SATURDAY MORNING, VENDORS
and customers stir early. It might still be dark or cold and windy, but
when it's Saturday morning, it's all about another big day at the market. From my spot in Maple Ridge Farm's booth in the north wing of
shed two, I had a view of the eastern sky as its gray turned to an orange-
pink around the skyscrapers of Detroit.

"Pretty, huh?" I said to my friend Shannon as we wrestled our ban-
ners into position with ornery bungee cords.

"Yes!" she replied. "But we might have bad weather coming. You
know, 'Red sky in the morning…'"

I nodded and shrugged. Bad weather was all in a day's work here in
our country's oldest open farmer's market. In the summer, it's sweltering
weather in the concrete and steel city. Shannon's jars of Slow Jams pop
their seals from the heat. And in the winter, a stiff wind whips up from
the Detroit River, chilling our bones and setting our teeth to chatter.

My fingers were red and achy from the cold as they dug through
the chest freezer for beef tenderloin, smoked bacon, or a nine-piece cut
chicken to display for purchase for our many passersby.

As the morning inched toward 7:00, the surrounding booths filled
with folding tables and a medley of vendors and wares. The small shops
opened around the perimeter of the market. The parking lots jammed
and the center aisles of the sheds became noisy pedestrian highways.

On my immediate left, Mr. Lore busily handed out samples of

his famous chess pies. Ethel's Edibles sold their delicious Pecan Sandies. Great Lakes Coffee was always freshly roasted, and Danielle in the Urban Grounds coffee car made an excellent Eye Opener with it. There was Pasta and Pasta, McClure's Pickles, The Spice Miser, Golden Wheat bakery, Drought organic beverages, and ever so much more.

Customers took samples of Farm Country cheese and homemade granola from my display. They bobbed their heads in definite approval as I told them about the benefits of our healthy meat. I enjoyed it when they came back for more week after week.

"This cheese is to die for," they would say. Or, "I have to come here for your granola. I send it to my sister in Oregon. She can't do without it."

I loved telling them about our Cow Share Program—a legal way for them to enjoy the benefits of raw milk.

"I get so excited when I see you bringing my jug of milk from the ice chest," a Cow Share owner told me.

"I can't wait to start chugging it," said another.

One man poured a generous amount of cream straight from the jug into his travel mug of black coffee. He then moved off into the crowd with his precious share of the milk from our cows on Maple Ridge Farm.

Customers strolled by in groups, in pairs, in families, or alone. They came from all over the world—France, Denmark, New Orleans, and New York. Eastern Market is a famous spot and a huge tourist attraction. Every week there would be wide-eyed people who would say, "This is the first time I've been here. Where do I start?"

Thousands of people are in that enormous, sprawling market, and there I was, a young Amish girl. But I loved it. I loved Shannon and my other vendor friends. I loved the diversity, the conglomeration, and the people.

I even loved the questions. Once, after explaining to an Iraqi who the Amish are, Shannon asked, "Don't you get tired of the questions? I mean, everyone is always so curious."

"You know," I told her, "I don't blame their wondering. I understand that to them we look, well, *weird*. There are so many misunderstand-ings about our culture that all these questions are a way I can give a fairer picture of us. But I have a reason for being different. Being a Christian impacts every area of my life. It's my life, so no, I don't mind talking about it."

I won't pretend though, that all the questions are easy ones. I give answers about my headcovering, technology, simple living, Amish youth, and our distinctive dress. I enjoyed describing a traditional Amish wedding meal to my friend Christina, who is an event plan-ner. I told one lady that "Amish" is not necessarily synonymous with "organic."

One type of question I always find tough is, "Is this Amish cheese?" or "Do you have Amish eggs?" My customers were not always inter-ested in a long-winded explanation on whether or not the chickens live an Amish lifestyle, or just a chicken lifestyle on a farm owned by an Amish family.

Often in the vast crowds I feel small and helpless, observing the spiritual warfare and crying voids in American society. Encounters with my customers, conversations with people I meet, and questions they ask make my answers feel insignificant—like a lone star in a night sky.

Then it dawned on me that one country girl cannot satisfactorily answer all the questions of seven billion people worldwide, or 40 thou-sand at Eastern Market, or even for my best friend. That takes faith in Jesus Christ, and His redemptive, empowering grace.

It takes living, boot leather testimonies to bring many lives one step closer to the God who is the Truth. That is what gives my life purpose.

Penny

Luke Weaver

And Adam gave names to all cattle, and to the fowl of the air, and to every beast of the field; but for Adam there was not found an help meet for him (Genesis 2:20).

THE MORNING SUNSHINE SENT HEAT WAVES SHIMMERING ACROSS THE pavement as our tiny buggy rattled along. I was ten years old and had the back of the buggy all to myself this morning. Mom and Dad were up front. We were on our way to help unload the belongings of a family who had moved into our community from Iowa.

Only a few months had gone by since we were newcomers to Michigan ourselves, having moved there from Missouri. I was wondering if the new family had a boy close to my age. They lived about four miles from where we did, off a dusty gravel road. I could see a few buggies were already there as we drove in. The truck with their household items hadn't arrived yet, so everyone sat under a tree and visited while we waited.

Soon a red semi pulling a trailer rumbled slowly up the road. The top of the trailer scraped a few tree branches as the driver eased into the lane. With a *whoosh* from the airbrakes, he parked close to the house.

Both cab doors swung open and a Mennonite man climbed down from the driver's side. From the passenger side, a boy who was surely close to my age jumped down. He grinned and waved a tanned arm. In a flash, he scampered around the back of the trailer ahead of the Mennonite man. The back end of the trailer was stacked high with boxes, wooden crates, and a few bales of straw. On top were some chickens in a wire cage, and beside their cage, a dog carrier.

The boy nimbly scrambled up the back of the trailer. He stood on his tiptoes, and, holding tight to a straw bale with one hand, he opened the carrier door with the other hand. A little black and tan Beagle looked out, wagging its tail rapidly, whimpering for joy, no doubt glad the long ride was over.

The boy laughed and beckoned to the dog with his arm, "Come, come." The little dog looked down and hesitated. "Come down," the boy pleaded, and the little dog jumped right into the crook of his elbow. In a flash, the boy let go of the straw bale, hopped to the ground, and set the overjoyed dog down.

"Hi there," the boy said as he skipped over to where I stood.

"Hi," I returned. "Did you have a long ride?"

"Sure did," he replied. "We left Iowa in the afternoon and drove all night. I liked riding in a semi, but I'm glad we're here."

The little dog trotted over, "This is Penny," he said, and bent down to pat her back. She hadn't stopped wagging her tail since getting off the trailer. Now she looked up at me and wrinkled one side of her lip to show her teeth. It looked like she was trying to smile.

"Penny," I said, and stroked her short little ears. She showed her gratefulness with more wagging and rubbed against my leg.

It seemed like Penny liked people because she then trotted over to the group of neighbors and "smiled" at everyone, wagging her tail all the while.

Soon we started to unload the truck. The household items were in boxes of varying sizes, so we formed a line and simply passed boxes from person to person. Someone removed a window from the basement and box after box of canned goods was squeezed through the space.

By lunchtime everything was unloaded except a few small boxes in the cab of the semi. Everyone washed up at the sink and got in line to fill up their plates. Almost everyone ate outside under the trees, because the day was clear and sunny with only a mild breeze. Penny was sound asleep in the middle of the group, her head between her front paws, the picture of contentment.

I heard somebody laugh and looked over to see everyone point at Penny. On top of her head was a toy helmet with the "D" of the Detroit

Tigers. Penny liked baseball, it seemed, because she only peered out from beneath the helmet, wagged her tail, and went back to sleep.

The next Sunday the little doggie came to church too. She smiled and begged to be petted. Everyone smiled back even though it was unusual for a dog to come to church. Penny soon became a regular guest at church and all other community gatherings. She simply trotted along behind the buggy wherever her family went.

Anyone who took a minute to say hello was her friend for life. Cries of delight from the toddlers usually welcomed her on Sunday morning. One Sunday our white-haired minister pointed out lessons from the life of the apostle Paul.

"We can see from Paul's epistles that he loved everyone he met. You know, maybe it's like that little dog that comes to church so often. She loves everyone, and no one is left out," he said with a smile.

One winter day our English neighbor Bob drove up in his black Ford. On his lap, looking over the wheel, was Penny. For once it seemed someone didn't like her. The neighbor across the road fed wild deer, and Penny would run over and bark at them. The neighbor didn't appreciate his deer being chased off. "Get rid of her, or else!" he warned.

And so, for the sake of neighborly peace, Penny's family asked if we would take her. We were delighted, of course. We always had a dog or two around, and Penny was a perfect addition.

This was of course no easy choice for the family. One of their sons had died in a farm accident some years earlier. Just before they left Iowa, they had all visited his grave site. When they arrived, two little beagle pups were sitting on the grave. One ran away, and the other one was Penny.

And so this very special dog came to live with us. She was about a year old that winter of 1998. The following spring, five puppies arrived, followed soon after by litters of seven and eight. Twenty puppies in less than two years was too many, so when Wendy, our neighbor, offered to take her to the vet to be fixed, we made an appointment and off she went. Penny was delighted with the truck ride and the new friends she made at the vet's office. By then she liked to ride in anything that had wheels, as long as she could see out.

Over the next few years Penny gained a little weight and continued to make a lot of new friends. Seemingly, she had an agreement with the local UPS driver, because she would wait right outside the truck door while the driver took the packages inside. Before he left, the driver would toss out a treat, and Penny would happily trot off with her prize.

When we had chicken for supper, Penny loved to eat the scraps. Often she would carry off the bones to bury somewhere. Usually it was in the garden. The dirt was soft, which meant it was easy to dig. Much to Mom's dismay, she would often find the bones the next spring when she planted peas or radishes.

In the winter of 2003, Penny adopted a more sedentary lifestyle. She slept behind the woodstove, which became her favorite pastime. Dad's recliner was another favorite spot. She no longer ran along behind the buggy, but started to ride inside. As soon as we'd start to hitch up, Penny would begin to whimper and plead until she was lifted into the buggy. She wanted the door to be open enough for her to look out. This made an unusual sight, as Dad's old, slow, "retirement horse" clomped along with Penny's head peering out the side.

Sometimes when we visited neighbors, she got confused about where she was or would become too busy at play to go home. When this happened, Penny seemed to know where all the married siblings lived. She would go to the nearest one's doorstep. They would hear a little scratch and open the door to see Penny wag her tail apologetically. She seemed to say, "Sorry to bother you, but could I stay here for the night?" They would make a little bed on the floor and Penny would gratefully curl up and go to sleep. They would leave a message for us and the next day we would pick her up.

Along with her sedentary lifestyle, she developed a fondness for people's food. And not healthy food, either. Cookies, ice cream, chips, you name it. If we ate it, Penny begged to try some. Our attempts to make sure she ate enough real dog food became a challenge.

For example, she once stayed overnight at my sister Myriad's house. Mom and Dad had dropped in to say hello, and Penny was too busy at play with Rob and Myriad's hyperactive cocker spaniel named Jake to notice when they left.

The next morning they offered her a dish of dog food for breakfast. They said she sniffed it a little and turned up her nose. They then mixed in a handful of crumbled Oreos, and that did wonders. Rob declared, "She ate the whole thing and then licked the bowl!"

As the years went by, life continued to be one big party for Penny and her two doggie buddies we had acquired: a snorting pug named Duke and a long-eared basset named Jean.

Salesmen, the mailman, friends, and neighbors, all were welcomed by that motley trio. None of these canines ever thought of being watchdogs. Any burglar would have been welcomed with wags and smiles, just the same as anyone else. Especially if he had Oreos.

Most of my nieces and nephews can credit at least part of their ability to walk with Penny. Her back was the perfect height for them to grab on and pull themselves up. She patiently took small steps as they tottered along. All of them adored her and would play with her for hours.

The last two years of Penny's life were marked by declining health. The first sign of her age was her hearing loss. Then the effort to get up onto Dad's recliner became an ordeal. She would stand in front of the recliner, look up, and take a step forward or back, trying to gauge the distance. Then with all the effort she could muster, up she went. Sometimes another jump would be required to make it. Once upon the cushion, she would sigh with relief and settle down for a long nap.

Then she developed diabetes, and we all knew she couldn't hang on much longer. None of us could bear the thought of parting with her because she had been a part of our lives for so many years. We tried to keep her comfortable with a nice soft bed and a few extra treats. But around Christmastime of 2012, a few sore spots on her leg and flanks simply would not heal. The sores began to bleed, which was certainly not a good sign.

Regretfully, we all knew that the time had come. Penny suffered and no longer enjoyed life. Kindly, our neighbor and friend Terri took Penny on one last ride. Penny had enjoyed many rides in Terri's minivan. Our local vet wrapped Penny in a soft blanket, where she went to sleep.

Thus ended Penny's long and fulfilling life. If a dog's life can be lived well, Penny's life qualified. Her memory lives on in the hearts of our family, as evidenced by this eulogy of sorts written by two of my nieces. At my mom and dad's place, the fridge is sort of a media hub. The doors are covered with a dry erase whiteboard, and it serves well for announcements, poems, and quotes from favorite authors. The girls wrote this the week after Penny left us:

Dear Penny,

We miss you very much and we wish you could come back soon. Please come back. Oh please! But you won't. Don't worry. This evening you aren't walking and trotting around in the kitchen eating Mommy's cookies. We love you very, very, very much. We still miss you because we liked to play with you. Penny, you can just live in our hearts.

Bye-bye, Penny. Bye-bye!

Under Arrest

Omer Miller

*For rulers are not a terror to good works, but to the evil. Wilt
thou then not be afraid of the power? do that which is good,
and thou shalt have praise of the same (Romans 13:3).*

OUR DRIVER'S MINIVAN HUMMED ALONG THE CANADIAN HIGHWAY ONE
hot summer afternoon. My traveling companions were the rest of the
ministry of our community. We had spent the day attending a meeting in Aylmer, Ontario, and were now on our way home.

I reclined the seat and tried to relax, relieved to be heading home.
I closed my eyes for what seemed a mere moment, only to be awakened with a start. The rumbling sounds of the Ambassador Bridge at
the border crossing into Port Huron, Michigan, interrupted my siesta.
The sight that greeted my tired eyes caused my heart to sink. There
were long lines of traffic backed up by each of the border patrol booths.

"We might as well settle down for a long wait," I announced. The
only answers I got behind me were long sighs of resignation. Our anticipated three-hour drive suddenly looked like four hours.

Slowly, we crept toward the border patrol booth. Finally, after we'd
inched along for half an hour, we stopped by the booth.

Our driver rolled down his window, ready for the rapid-fire questions. "Where are you from? Are you U.S. citizens? Where are you
going? Where have you been? What for? How long were you there?"

Our driver patiently answered the questions and tried not to irri-
tate the officer or cause any undue suspicion. We didn't want to sacrifice more time than necessary, anxious to get home to our families.
My son James handed his personal identification papers ahead to the
driver. The young officer took them and began to punch his computer.

We patiently waited for him to return our papers and send us on our way.

"He sure is taking his time," Deacon Omer Schrock noted. The officer didn't peck away at his computer anymore but rather ignored us. Suddenly, out of nowhere our vehicle was surrounded by armed guards. My heart jumped in my throat.

"What's up with this?" James exclaimed. What a sight! Here were five harmless Amish ministers surrounded by security guards who brandished their weapons as though we were some serial killers.

One guard stepped up to my door, jerked it open. "Get out!" he commanded. I got out and stood beside the van, unsure how to respond.

"Raise your hands above your head," he barked.

I quickly complied. My mind refused to believe this.

"Walk toward the officer over there," he continued.

I walked toward another officer ten feet behind the minivan, my hands high above my head. A hot wind blew and tousled my hatless head. It also threw my long, graying beard over my shoulder.

The officer glared at me as I approached him. "Turn around," he snapped. "Lower your hands behind your back."

I obeyed.

Instantly I heard an ominous *click*. I was handcuffed.

"Walk to the building to your right," he ordered. Just in case this gray-haired Amish bishop decided to make a break, he moved me along with his Glock.

Suddenly my mind caught up with the events of the last two minutes. I was under arrest! So were my companions, including my son. What a welcome into our own country! Now I knew how our Anabaptist forefathers felt when they were arrested for no crime.

As we moved toward the building, the officer and I had to cross several busy traffic lanes.

This is quite a sight, I thought as I imagined tomorrow's newspaper headlines would read, "Amish Men Arrested at Border." At this point I felt more curiosity than fear, so I asked the officer, "What's going on?"

"Keep on moving," he demanded, and didn't miss a step. The officer wasn't very communicative so I kept further thoughts to myself.

We entered the building where I was directed into a small room and released from my uncomfortable handcuffs. I raised my hands while I received a vigorous pat down.

"Take off your shoes and empty your pockets. Put your things into this basket." He pointed to a small basket.

Meanwhile, unknown to me, the other four brethren were receiving the same treatment. As one of the brothers was moved toward the building, he heard the officer mutter, "I think this is a mistake."

After 30 minutes my officer instructed me to put on my shoes and he returned my personal belongings.

I was reunited with my fellow travelers in another room. The officer in charge apologized profusely and explained what happened. "When James Miller's name came up on the computer," he explained, "it showed he was a wanted man and considered dangerous. Obviously, we caught the wrong James Miller." They had thought my son was a dangerous and wanted man. How ironic.

The rookie officer in the booth had taken no chances and pushed the emergency button, which caused this exciting scene. Fortunately, the driver wasn't arrested but was instructed to drive his vehicle to a certain spot where they X-rayed it.

After the excitement died down and everyone understood what happened, the officers were friendly and apologetic and wished us well. In turn we recognized them for doing their duty and assured them we were not offended.

"We pray for our government officials daily," we told them. The officers thanked us and wished us well.

Thus ended an unforgettable experience that reminded us that but for the grace of God, we could live in a land where we do not have our freedom.

The Victory

Kenneth Gingerich

*Jesus answered and said unto him, Verily, verily, I
say unto thee, Except a man be born again, he
cannot see the kingdom of God (John 3:3).*

I WAS 16 YEARS OLD AND STOOD THAT EVENING WITH MY BACK TO THE
sun, shifting my weight from one foot to the other.

From the crest of the small hill I could see out across the valley
polka-dotted with woods and neat little farmsteads. Even in the growing dusk it wasn't hard to see that the pastures, woods, and everything
was responding with lush fervor to spring's call.

A coyote howled in the distance, and I shifted my weight again. I
tightened my arms across my chest in an attempt to relieve the pressure within. I was way too disturbed to head for bed and relax. Instead,
I was standing out here in an attempt to sort out my thoughts.

Today our community had held their semiannual practice of com-
munion. The sermons had seemed to speak directly to me all day. I
had sat spellbound as the ministers had gone through the Old Testament stories. And finally the preaching had climaxed in the afternoon
with the account of the sufferings and death of Jesus. This had especially stood out to me and apparently to the rest of the congregation.
We had all been spellbound as the bishop strode back and forth speaking of God's gift of salvation.

"The burden of sin used to lie heavily on me," the bishop had
preached. "It was torment. I would go to bed nights and couldn't sleep.
I was afraid of God. The thought of death terrified me. I couldn't go
on like that, so I persuaded myself to try harder. If I would do my best,
surely I could have victory over sin. Surely God would accept me if

He saw how hard I was trying, but no matter how hard I tried, I never could find peace. My best was not good enough. The works of the flesh had a hold on me and, as a result, I felt lost, condemned, and unsaved. Outwardly my life was good and in order; inwardly I lived a life of sin and impurity."

I had leaned forward to catch the bishop's every word.

"But friends," he had said, "this struggle all changed the day I received Christ into my life. Now I found it was possible to live a life of victory over sin. Out of ourselves we can't do anything good. We *can't* have victory over sin. We can try, but no matter how hard we try, we still can't."

The bishop had paused before the center aisle to point over the congregation. "Christ has already won the victory over sin on the cross. When He rose again He triumphed over all the powers of sin. Why do we even want to try and win a victory for ourselves when so perfect and final a victory has been won already? Christ did His part. Our part is to simply yield ourselves. Just commit your past, your failures, your temptations, whatever it may be to Him. He will take care of them all, and besides that Christ will give you the power and strength that you need to stand victorious over sin."

I had felt a keen sense of undoneness when the bishop had mentioned this. And again when the bishop had passed around the bread and wine. I felt a deep desire to belong to this faith. And yet I felt dirty and unclean. A pressing weight of guilt bore down on me. I knew I wasn't ready to die.

The coyote howled again, but I hardly noticed it. The struggle inside intensified. A voice spoke loudly that it would not be worth it. But another voice persisted, "Come unto Me and I will give you rest."

Suddenly I lifted my head as the thought came to me. Dad and Mom could help me.

When I went in the house, I approached Dad and asked, "What do I have to do to become a part of the church? I'm so tired of the way things have been going in my life the last while. I want something different."

Dad leaned forward. "Kenneth, you're asking questions that we all need to ask ourselves at one time or another. You asked what one must do. Well, you probably realize that unless Jesus is the Lord and Master of your life, church membership won't do you much good."

I looked down and said, "I know I'm going to need that victory over sin in my life the bishop talked about today. But how does one do this?"

Dad glanced over at Mom. "You don't know how happy it makes us to hear you say this, Kenneth. The first thing any of us need to do is realize the sin in our life and that of ourselves we are lost. If you understand this, then you're ready to confess your sins to God and ask Him to come into your life. Do you feel you're ready?"

"Yes, Dad. That's what I want," I said boldly.

"Would you like to pray and ask God to come into your life?" Dad asked.

"Yes," I said, and so we did.

Later I sat on the edge of my bed and a happy sigh escaped me. I felt so relieved and happy. It was a wonderful feeling after being weighed down with sin and guilt for so long. I picked up the Bible and read the references Dad had given me.

The first one was Matthew 3:8: "Bring forth therefore fruits worthy of repentance."

The next one was Acts 26:20: "That they should repent and turn to God, and do works meet for repentance."

This is just a start tonight, I realized. Once again I knelt down and thanked God for the gift of salvation. I also asked for help to continue to be a good soldier of the cross.

My Journey to Baptism

Kenneth Gingerich

*Then Peter said unto them, Repent, and be baptized every
one of you in the name of Jesus Christ for the remission of sins,
and ye shall receive the gift of the Holy Ghost (Acts 2:38).*

EASY, CHARGER. EASY, BOY." I PLACED MY FOOT INTO THE STIRRUP AND
swung myself onto the bay gelding. "Okay, boy. Let's go."

As the horse cantered out the lane I sat back and relaxed. It was a
beautiful morning. The birds sang, the flowers bloomed, and the warm
spring breezes felt good on my face. It was a wonderful morning in
more ways than one.

This is how it feels to be at peace with God, I thought as I steered Charger down the road toward Bishop Leroy Hershberger's place.

When I pulled in the lane, I dismounted and walked slowly toward
the house, a trifle nervous.

I gave the door several raps. Leroy opened the door and greeted me
with, "Why, good morning, Kenneth. I didn't even hear you drive in."

"I rode Charger since he's feeling plenty frisky this time of the year
anyway," I said.

Leroy chuckled. "No doubt the weather this morning is enough to
make anyone frisky." He moved inside the house to point to a hook.
"Just hang your hat there and come on in. Anna and the girls went to
clean a neighbor's house this morning so we have the place to ourselves."
He pulled out a chair from the table and motioned for me to sit.

We talked about this and that for a while. It was easy to talk to the
bishop. Finally he leaned forward and said, "Well, your dad said you
have some things on your mind that you'd like to discuss."

I shuffled my feet. "Yes, I guess...um...I was thinking about instruction class. I'd like to become a part of the church." I ran my fingers through my hair and groped for words.

Leroy nodded and looked kindly at me. "What makes you feel like that?"

I bit the inside of my cheek. "Well, the other day I talked with my parents about the condition of my soul and they explained things to me and I had this experience where I gave my heart to God. And now I desire to become a part of the church."

"I'm so glad for you," Leroy said. "This is something that causes even the angels in heaven to rejoice." He was silent for a moment. "But Ken, before we can accept you for instruction we need to see that you have proven yourself. The church requires her members to walk a pure, holy life apart from the world and sin. So before we take someone into the church we want him to prove worthy of the responsibilities that lie ahead of him. Now don't get me wrong; we don't look for perfect members, nor do we expect anybody to prove himself by his own strength. Only as we give ourselves to God as a living sacrifice can we be transformed by the renewing of our minds and walk a pure and holy life. So let me ask you how things have been going the last while, especially in your personal life."

"Well," I began slowly, "there's been a struggle. I've failed quite often, though there are also times when I'm victorious."

Leroy thought a bit before he answered. "You know, you don't need to feel ashamed of your confession. You aren't different from the rest of us. Many struggle because they don't open up. So far, I'm encouraged with what you've said. Openness is a vital ingredient in order for us to help each other. The members in the church aren't perfect," he continued. "Failures do happen, but they must be dealt with. This is the church's responsibility. But we've discovered that it helps a lot for young people to grow stronger first, before they make that serious commitment to God and His church." His eyes glistened with compassion. "So why don't we take some more time? Maybe this fall we can take a look again. In the meantime spend time with God every day, study the Word, and allow Him to continue working in your life. Also stay open to your parents. Be accountable to them. If you struggle, talk it over with them."

I nodded and rose from the chair. "Thanks for your time and the encouragement. I do want to be an upstanding church member."

Leroy arose and said, "Nourish that desire, my boy. Allow it to direct you, and with God's help someday you will be a good church member. I look forward with you to the day when you can take this step."

I told the bishop goodbye and left. The sun had grown warmer as I turned Charger toward home. The way ahead suddenly seemed clearer than it had before.

It won't be easy, I thought. But I knew that with Christ beside me and this goal before me, the day would come. A feeling of joy washed over me as I galloped into our lane.

Life as a Christian that summer wasn't always easy. Sometimes it was more difficult than I had imagined. But then the peace and joy would return to my heart and I knew I wouldn't trade that feeling for anything. When I faced my temptations, God would send a warning by His Spirit through my mind. It was like a warning shot, and I knew I had to listen and resist. At times I was deeply disappointed in myself. The urge to sin was strong, and only the power of God could overcome it. I spoke with Dad and Mom often about my struggles.

Mom once told me, "Welcome to the Christian life."

I wondered if had heard correctly. I had no idea she had her struggles too.

"I'm glad you're sensitive about this," Mom continued. "We always need to be sensitive about the things we do wrong. And I'm glad you came for help. We need each other."

"But why do I fail?" I asked.

"The flesh dies hard," Mom told me. "We need to die with Christ daily. It's something that needs to be done as long as we live in this body. And a man who thinks he is standing should take heed lest he fall. Satan is so tricky. We think we're on top and before we know it we fall for something we shouldn't."

I nodded, though I didn't really understand.

"We grow and learn as long as we live," Mom added. "Let each temptation be a stepping-stone instead of a stumbling block."

And so it went. At times God helped me out directly, and other times through others. A sudden relief would flood through my whole body as I knew that God understood my struggles and that He always provided a way of escape as I was willing to turn my back on sin.

Summer passed and fall arrived. I was back at the bishop's house again. He offered me a chair. The cold autumn rain lashed against the window panes. I knew that before long winter would envelop the landscape with its snowy grip.

"Care for some hot cocoa?" Leroy asked.

"Sure." I took the mug as the bishop settled down in his rocker.

"How did you find this summer, my boy?" Leroy asked.

"The Christian life is worth it, but I have much to learn," I said. "And I still desire to join the church, even if I feel unworthy."

"Sometimes we fail and sometimes we are victorious," Leroy said.

I looked up, startled. "How do you know that?"

"Because I've had experience with the Christian life too, and that's how I find it for myself," Leroy said with a smile. "The important thing is our desire to please God and to know His will for our lives and not let up. It needs to continue and grow. As time continues we discover that the victory Jesus won over sin is becoming more and more a part of our lives."

"Yes, that's what I find," I agreed. "With God's help, along with my parents', I can be victorious."

"I'm glad to hear that." Leroy leaned forward. "So your desire to be part of the church is still the same?"

"Yes," I said. "I need the church and I want to do my part in supporting her as a faithful member."

"I will discuss this with the other ministers, then," Leroy said. "But I see no reason why you can't join the instruction class this fall."

A deep feeling of unworthiness filled me as I listened to the bishop's words. God had helped me this far, and God would help me onward. It was the only way I could go on.

Baptism
Kenneth Gingerich

*On hearing this, they were baptized in
the name of the Lord Jesus (Acts 19:5).*

AN EXPECTANT HUSH FILLED THE CROWDED HOUSE. THE CLOCK'S HAND
pointed at 10:30 as Bishop Leroy slowly rose to his feet. He glanced
along the many rows of men and women sitting on the backless
wooden benches. They all looked at him with expectation. Finally the
bishop's gaze rested on the front benches where three boys and two girls
sat with solemn faces.

I was on the front bench that day seated between the other two boys.
It won't be long now, I thought. This was the day I had so long looked
forward to. I would be baptized. Somehow the nervousness I expected
wasn't in my heart. Instead, I felt a peace and even joy.

Bishop Leroy began to speak on the meaning of baptism and church
membership. From there he moved on to the account in Acts where the
first church was founded on the day of Pentecost after Peter's sermon.
The bishop spoke in a simple style, straightforward. In his earnestness
he sometimes forgot himself and strode back and forth in front of the
other ministers. I too became taken up in his message.

"We do not need to go to prison for our faith today, as our forefathers did," the bishop said. "But that doesn't mean we aren't tried for
our faith. You have probably already discovered that there are still trials and temptations in our lives. That won't change just because you are
baptized. Trials and temptations are something we must face as long as
we live. This is how we are often tried for our faith today. But with the
help of God we can be victorious."

The hands on the clock continued to move steadily. I shifted on the bench and bowed my head. Yes, I knew this was true. The way of the Christian wasn't always easy. But God had not let me down even once. Even if I failed, God had always been there to take me back.

As the bishop went deeper into his sermon a hush settled over the congregation. The time of the baptism drew near. The bishop finally came to the story of Philip and the eunuch in the book of Acts.

"Here is water; what doth hinder me to be baptized?" the eunuch had asked.

Philip told him, "If thou believest with all thine heart, thou mayest."

"I believe that Jesus Christ is the Son of God," the eunuch responded.

And Philip had taken the eunuch down to the water and baptized him on his confession of faith.

Bishop Leroy paused and looked at us. "Dear young people, if you desire to make this confession of the eunuch your own, you may kneel before the congregation."

A calm filled my heart as I knelt with the others.

The bishop asked us the questions.

"Do you believe that Jesus Christ is the Son of the God?"

"Yes," we all answered.

"Do you recognize this to be a Christian church and fellowship under which you now submit yourselves?"

"Yes."

"Do you renounce the world, the devil with all his subtle ways, your own flesh and blood, and desire to serve Jesus Christ alone, who died on the cross for you?"

"Yes."

"Do you promise before God and the church that you will support these teachings and regulations with the Lord's help, faithfully attend the services of the church, help to counsel and work in the church, and not forsake it whether this leads to life or death?"

"Yes," we all answered in unison.

Bishop Leroy gazed across the crowd. "You have heard their vows. Let's rise for prayer."

The congregation stood while we stayed on our knees. Little

children craned their necks to see better. I straightened my back as my turn came and the hands of the bishop cupped on my head.

"Upon your confession of faith, made before God and these many witnesses, I baptize you in the name of the Father, the Son, and the Holy Spirit. Amen."

Tiny rivulets of water ran down my face and dropped on the floor as the deacon poured. I squeezed my eyes shut. A tear threatened to join the water on the floor. Behind me, I heard Mom blow her nose while Dad huskily cleared his throat. It was indeed a solemn moment. Here I was, an unworthy member of the bride of Christ.

"Oh God," I prayed silently, "help me stay faithful whether it leads to life or death. And Father, thank You for providing victory over sin."

The Buggy Wreck

Titus Yoder

*Thou wilt keep him in perfect peace, whose mind is stayed
on thee: because he trusteth in thee (Isaiah 26:3).*

PING! TEACHER TIMOTHY TAPPED THE LITTLE BELL ON HIS DESK SIGNAL-
ing the end of another school day. With much rustling we pupils put
our books away, ready to be dismissed.

Fifth grader Andrew took the wastebasket around to collect the
various scraps we had accumulated during the day. When Andrew finished he returned to his seat and we all rose to join our two teachers in
a parting song. Another tap on the bell signaled our dismissal and we
all filed out to the cloakroom in chaotic lines.

"Larry," I said as we went out, "it's our turn to bring in wood. Let's
see if we can be done before our sisters finish sweeping the classroom."
I grabbed the wheelbarrow and we headed for the woodshed.

A few wheelbarrow loads later, we had the wood box filled, but the
girls were already finished sweeping. I went back out to get our horse
ready to go home. First, I used a scoop shovel and carefully cleaned
out his stall before I threw his droppings on the manure pile behind
the barn. Next, I got his bridle, pulled it over his head, and buckled it
around his neck. Then, I led him from his stall to our buggy. Soon, I had
him hitched up and held on to his bridle while I waited for my sisters.

"You're a good boy, Nicky," I murmured as I scratched his neck.
"What would we do without such a faithful old horse like you?"

The school door slammed and I saw my three sisters rushing out.
We all squeezed into our single-seated buggy and drove out on the lane.

"I got a hundred percent on my arithmetic test today!" second
grader Anna Mary squealed as we started down the road.

"Oh, good for you. That's always a nice feeling, isn't it?" sixth grader Rebecca praised her. "On my last one, I got a ninety-six percent and thought I did quite well."

"It's the English tests that always cause me problems," I said. "I've gotten a one hundred percent in arithmetic, but if I could get one in English I'd be tickled pink. Usually I have a hard time even reaching ninety-one or ninety-two percent."

"Amy looked so funny today," laughed third grader Joanna. "We were cutting out pictures in art class and she was really concentrating on being careful. What looked so funny was the way she kept opening and closing her mouth along with her scissors."

"That would have been funny," chuckled Rebecca as she leaned out of the buggy to wave at our classmates Susan and Anna, who came out of the driveway of the little bulk food store run by Beth Yoder.

"Oh dear, now they'll probably pass us," I muttered. "I wish this old plod was safe and fast instead of safe and slow."

Sure enough, in no time at all they caught up with us and whipped past with mischievous grins.

"My, their horse is feeling good," Joanna remarked. Then she gasped, "Oh, no! Look!"

Up ahead the speeding buggy was rocking violently to one side and then the other. Through the back window the girls' heads and arms were seen wildly bobbing and flailing. A leg poked out the door and disappeared again. The snap-down curtain in the back popped open and groceries flew out. A pack of frozen blueberries burst and bounced in all directions. With a final vicious sway, the buggy crashed onto its left side and slid to a stop. In its wake it left scattered groceries, a head covering, a shoe, and one very rumpled looking girl lying in a little heap.

"Whoa, Nicky!" I yelled as I pulled him to a stop. "Joanna and Anna Mary, you watch him while we go help."

Rebecca and I hopped out and ran up to the wreckage just as another rumpled person appeared at the door, which was now on top. It was Susan and she clambered out to limp back to Anna, who was still lying on the road. "Oh, Anna! Are you okay?" she sobbed.

"I don't know," Anna groaned, easing up to a sitting position. "I think so. Nothing feels broken."

Seeing that no one was critically hurt, I turned my attention to their horse. Fortunately, he hadn't panicked in the hubbub but stood still, seemingly bewildered by the sudden turn of events. With Susan's help I managed to get him unhitched and away from the buggy. Then Susan helped Anna hobble back up the road to the store where they cleaned up a bit and bandaged their cuts and scrapes.

By now their father, Greg, had appeared. He had been summoned by Ron, a neighbor who had witnessed the accident. He raced off in his pickup to the sawmill where Greg worked and brought him over.

"Where are the girls? Are they all right?" he asked.

"Yes, they're okay," I said. "They're at the store. They've got some bruises and scratches, but aren't seriously hurt."

He checked up on them and was soon back. "We'll need to get this buggy off the road," he said. "Ron, can we put it on your trailer to haul it home?"

Ron got his trailer and with a heave and a shove the buggy was set up and rolled onto the trailer. It was discovered that one side of the shafts had broken loose and that was what caused the buggy to go out of control and tip over.

Once everything was taken care of, we siblings all piled into our buggy once more and with faithful, steady Nicky plodding along, we continued our drive home.

"Maybe a slow horse isn't so bad after all," I mused. "They probably wouldn't have tipped if they hadn't been going so fast."

On our arrival home, Mom met us at the door. "Are you all okay?" she asked. "It kept getting later and later and then I saw Ron go past with a bashed-up buggy."

"Yes, we're fine," we chorused. Then we all proceeded to tell her what happened.

Once Mom got the story straight she shook her head and said, "My, you did have some excitement! Thank God nobody was seriously hurt." Then she grinned at me and added, "I'm also glad that we have a nice slow horse for you children."

Christmas Caroling

Joanna Yoder

For unto you is born this day in the city of David a
Saviour, which is Christ the Lord (Luke 2:11).

I CAREFULLY FASTENED A BIG GREEN BOW ON TOP OF THE BREAD BAG
with a piece of Scotch tape. Then I chose a smaller white bow and taped
it to the side of the jar of apple butter. I stood back to survey my work.
"That looks good," I decided. "Now to get a card ready…"

Tonight my brother Titus and my sister Rebecca and I planned to
go Christmas caroling along with the rest of the youth. We had been
asked to take along a plate of goodies to leave at one of the places where
we would sing. At Mom's suggestion, I had decided to take a loaf of
the bread she had made that afternoon and a pint of homemade apple
butter.

I hurried to the desk and got the box of Christmas cards. I picked a
card with a picture of a baby in a manger. On the inside I wrote, "Dear
Friends, may you have a blessed Christmas! From the Evart Amish
Youth Group." I taped the card to the side of the loaf of bread and
placed everything in a small box. There! Now I needed to get myself
ready.

I went into my bedroom and opened the closet door. Which dress
should I wear, dark green or light blue?

I grabbed the blue. *This one is so cheery, just like Christmas*, I thought,
so excited for tonight's adventure. I loved singing Christmas carols.
And it was even more fun to sing them with my friends.

A few minutes later I hurried into the kitchen. Titus was sitting at
the table eating a toasted cheese sandwich. He said, "Joanna, you better hurry. I'm about ready to go."

"I know," I said.

"Joanna, do you want a sandwich too?" Mom asked.

"Yes, but wrap it in foil so I can eat it on the way," I said. "I still have to comb my hair."

"Where are you going?" four-year-old Esther asked.

"To the community building," I answered. "All the youth are meeting there, and then we're going caroling. There'll be four wagons, but we'll split into two groups. That way we'll be able to sing for more people."

"I wish I could go," 12-year-old Wilma sighed.

I grinned at her. "You only have four more years to wait."

"Are you dressing warmly?" Mom asked as she handed me the sandwich. "There's a sharp wind."

"I certainly feel warm enough right now," I said. "And thanks for the sandwich."

I wrapped my scarf around my neck, pulled on my boots and gloves, and grabbed my sandwich and the box with bread and apple butter. "'Bye, everyone!" I called.

A chorus of goodbyes echoed back. "Have a good evening," Mom called after us.

"Think of me," 15-year-old Anna Mary said dolefully.

I laughed. "Cheer up! You can go along next year." I shut the door behind me and hurried to the buggy.

It didn't take long to drive the two miles to the community building. Once there, I helped Titus unhitch the horse and hurried into the cloakroom.

"Good evening," I greeted the other girls as I took off my boots. "Emma, here's what I brought along for a goodies plate." I held the box with bread in it.

"Good," she answered. "Once everyone is here we'll have to make sure each group has the right number of plates," she answered.

"Who is going along as parents?" I asked Barbara.

"Nathans and Mahlons," she answered. "And Melvins will stay here to make supper for us."

I nodded. "I think I already smell something good."

"Who are we waiting for?" Ida asked.

"Everyone's here except Mahlons," Ruth answered.

Emma looked out the window. "I think they're coming right now."

Sure enough, a minute later they burst through the door. Before long everyone had gathered in the women's cloakroom so they could give us further directions. Melvins were the youth leaders and had arranged everything for the evening, including notifying people so they would know to expect us.

"I'll read off the ones going with the Mahlons' group." Melvin proceeded to read off a list of names. "The rest will go with Nathans'." He paused, then continued. "In the front of your songbook is a paper telling who your group will be singing for and who starts which song. After you've been at each of the places, we'll gather here for supper. Try to be back by eight thirty."

Nearly 40 youth pulled on their boots and hurried out the door. I headed for Nathans' wagon with seven other girls.

"Is there room for everyone?" Mattie, Nathan's wife, asked from the front seat.

"Some of us can sit on the back," Miriam said as she settled herself on the back of the wagon, dangling her feet over the edge. I plopped down beside her, and with a jerk we were off.

"It feels like we could slide off," said Marietta, who was sitting with us. "If I start sliding, I'll grab you and take you with me."

I reached under the seat behind us. "I can take hold of a bar that's under the seat," I said. "I don't think I'll fall off, so if you start sliding just grab hold of me."

As we settled that issue, the horse trotted briskly down the road. Behind us came another wagon. A cold wind blew, piling the snow into drifts and blasting snow into our faces.

"We thought about putting off the caroling because of the weather," Miriam said.

"I'm glad you didn't," I declared. "This weather just makes it more adventurous. I'm glad we have snow."

"Me too," agreed Ruth. "Last year when we went caroling we hardly had any snow, and it was so muddy. It didn't seem like Christmastime."

"I just hope no one gets too cold," Miriam said. "The temperature isn't so low, but the wind makes it feel cold."

"I'm not cold yet," I declared. "But I have lots of clothes on."

We continued to chat as the wagon rattled down the road. It wasn't long before the horse slowed down to turn into the driveway.

"This is Jesse Stewart's place, isn't it?" asked Regina.

"Yes," I answered. "We came here last year when we went caroling."

"Let's walk in the drive," Carol Ann said, jumping off the wagon. We all followed her example and walked up to the garage where we were sheltered from the wind. We waited as the men tied the horses.

Nathan went up to the door and knocked. Dogs yapped inside. Finally the door opened and then closed again. Nathan came over to us and opened the garage door. "He said we can go in through the garage," he explained.

We stepped back and let the boys go first. Miriam and I were the last to enter. As we turned to go down the stairs, Jesse stopped us. "Here's something for you." He held a package.

"Thank you," Miriam said, taking the brightly wrapped package before we followed the others down to the basement.

The boys lined up in a row and we girls formed another row in front of them. Jesse seated himself on a chair to listen.

"The first song we'll be singing is 'Christ Is Born in Bethlehem,'" Nathan announced. Someone started the song and the basement rang with the words.

After a few more songs, we sang our parting verse:

> *We wish you a blessed Christmas,*
> *We wish you a blessed Christmas,*
> *We wish you a blessed Christmas,*
> *And a happy new year!*

"Well, that's all the songs we picked," Nathan told Jesse. "Do you have any you'd like us to sing?"

"Oh no, no," the slim, elderly man said. "I'm happy with what you chose to sing. It was beautiful. Thank you for coming."

"We enjoyed it," Nathan said as we filed up the stairs.

We burst out into the cold and piled back on the wagons. I found a place beside Lois on the leather wagon seat.

"We're going to Eugene Shermann's next, aren't we?" Lois asked.

"Yes," I answered. "I'm glad our group is going there. I've never been there."

It wasn't long before we swung into the driveway at Eugene's. We girls huddled beside the garage where there was a little protection from the wind. Christmas lights hung above us from the eaves and twinkled on a bush.

Before long Nathan opened the garage door. We waited in the garage while he knocked on a door leading into a small entryway.

The door opened, and a stoop-shouldered gentleman appeared. "Come on in! We've been expecting you."

Everyone squeezed into the tiny entrance. Being one of the last to enter, I hesitated. Was there room for me? Carol Ann slid over on a chair and motioned for me to sit down.

Quickly I joined her. "Couldn't we sing better if we stood up?" I whispered.

"There's hardly room to stand up with this table and chairs in the way," she whispered.

"I guess you're right," I answered as I found the right page in my songbook.

Elmer started the first song and everyone joined in. It was uncomfortable to be so crowded, but the singing sounded nice in such a small room. I glanced at Eugene as he wiped a few tears. His petite wife sat on a chair beside him with a sweet smile on her face.

"Brightest and best of the sons of the morning!" Elmer started the second verse and I turned my attention to the songbook and put my all into the song.

We sang a few more songs then bade Eugene "Goodnight" and "blessed Christmas." One of the girls handed them a plate of home-made candy before we headed back out into the cold.

"Is it okay if I sit on your lap?" I asked JoEllen as I scrambled onto the wagon.

"Sure. Someone has to sit on a lap. You'll just keep me warm," she said.

So I did and we started off down the road again. The horse didn't go as fast as he had at first, but he kept up a steady pace.

"Brrr, it's colder when you're sitting on top," I said as I pulled my scarf over my nose.

Our next stop was at Tom Shaw's. Tom and Terry did taxi work for the Amish, so we knew them well. We filed into the kitchen and were soon heartily singing.

After the parting verse, Tom passed out cookies for everyone.

"Are you going to sing a song for us now?" Nathan teased.

"No, I can't sing," Tom chuckled.

I looked at the Christmas tree set up in the living room and the many Christmas decorations throughout the house as I munched on my cookie.

"Well, we'd better go," Nathan said a few minutes later. "Thanks for the cookies."

"You're welcome. Thanks for coming to sing, and also for these goodies." Tom held up the plate one of the girls had given him.

I added my own thanks as I turned to go outside.

We started off for our last stop. I listened to the chatter swirling around me and added my own two cents occasionally. How I enjoyed socializing with my friends!

The horse pulled in at Dirk Pattee's house and everyone hopped off.

"I'm going to leave my gloves on the wagon," I decided impulsively. "That way I won't have to hold them and my songbook while we're singing." I tossed my gloves under the seat and hurried to join the group of girls.

Nathan and Mattie led the way to the back door. Nathan knocked and we waited expectantly. He knocked again. Still no one answered the door.

"I'm going to try the front door," Nathan decided. He disappeared around the corner of the house.

"Do you think they aren't home?" JoEllen asked.

"We let them know we're coming," Miriam answered.

"I wish someone would answer the door. I'm ready to go inside where it's warm," I said.

"Maybe we'll have to stand out here to sing," Carol Ann said.

Just then Nathan reappeared around the corner of the house. "They're coming out," he told us.

Sure enough, the basement door opened and a middle-aged man and young boy stepped outside.

"This is going to be real caroling," Regina whispered as we stepped closer together to form a circle.

Miriam started the first song and everyone joined in. The song sounded small as it drifted away into the night. I pulled the cuffs of my coat over my hands and turned slightly so the yard light would shine on the words in the songbook. *Perhaps I should've worn my gloves after all*, I thought.

I glanced around at our little group, red-cheeked and cold but singing heartily. A gust of wind blew a shower of snow over us, and we moved closer together. My heart warmed. This was real caroling! Why, this was more adventurous than any of the other places had been. This was fun!

I turned my attention to the song and joined in with my whole heart.

After the parting verse, Dirk thanked us for coming, but no one lingered to visit.

"Let's start off running back to the community center," someone suggested.

"Yes, that would feel good and would warm us up," I agreed.

I grabbed my gloves off the wagon and joined the others to run out the driveway. We jogged down the road, but before long my side started to ache and I was relieved when a few of the others slowed to a walk.

It didn't take long to walk the rest of the way to the community building and we burst in the door to the bright warmth.

"Oh, it smells good in here!" I exclaimed as I unwrapped my scarf.

"I know. It makes me hungry just to smell supper," Miriam said.

Finally, I had my coat off and my boots placed beside the door. I sank down on a bench beside Ruth. "I'm ready to sit down and warm up," I commented.

"Me too," Miriam said. "I hope the other group comes soon so we can eat."

"Let's sing while we wait," someone suggested.

"Yes, let's," I agreed, and fetched my songbook from the shelf.

After a few songs the others burst in the door, red-cheeked and cold.

As soon as everyone had removed their wraps, we were seated at the long L-shaped table that had been set up. The lights were dimmed and the candles on the table lit. Small glass dishes filled with candy sparkled in the candlelight.

"Let's sing 'Come and Dine,' and then we'll have a silent prayer before we eat," Melvin said. The room was quiet as everyone bowed their heads, but at the *amen* the chatter started again.

Steaming bowls of chili were sent around the table followed by trays piled with individually wrapped hot ham and cheese sandwiches. A cup of hot chocolate was offered to everyone.

"This is just what we need to warm up," I said as I took a spoonful of chili.

"Were you really cold?" Rebecca asked.

"It wasn't so bad," I answered. "I got cold at the last place, but I wasn't chilled. I thought I was warmed up by the time we walked back here to the community building, but my toes hurt after I took off my boots so they must've been cold."

We described our adventures to the ones who were in the other group and they described their evening. Cinnamon rolls were sent around to top off the meal.

"These are from Eugene Shermann," Bertha said as she set a container of pretty cut-out cookies on the table.

"So that's what was in the package he gave to Miriam," I said as I picked out a star-shaped cookie.

After the delicious meal we girls quickly washed the dishes and pulled on our wraps once again.

"Goodnight!" I called to my friends as I headed outside to Titus's buggy.

Caroling was over for another winter, but a warm glow remained in my heart. It had been a worthwhile evening and we had made good memories.

The Amish FBI

Nathan Miller

*Beloved, believe not every spirit, but try the spirits
whether they are of God: because many false prophets
are gone out into the world (1 John 4:1).*

A NOTABLE TRAIT AMONG THE AMISH IS SIMPLICITY. THIS IS APPARENT
in several areas of life, but usually it's most evident in dress, vocation,
homes, and even health. No radios, television, or cars. Simplicity is also
evident in the way the Amish think. Amish people tend to trust others
and take things at face value, sometimes to their misfortune.

Amish people will not go to the doctor for every sneeze and sniffle,
which is a testament to their frugality. However, when sicknesses do
occur, age-old home remedies are applied, in which they combat one
illness after another. Garlic for colds, Unkers for congestion, prune
juice for constipation, and the chiropractor for everything else.

Unfortunately, down through the years certain health scams have
found their way into Amish homes and taken advantage of these fru-
gal and traditional folk.

Simplicity however doesn't exclude all new innovations. In many
Amish publications such as *Die Botshaft* or *Plain Interests*, distributors
hawk their latest cure-all products and devices. Some of these have
good qualities, while others arouse suspicion. And some health products call for more research than the cure-all tincture. These products,
regardless of their claims, do demand a certain strain on the Amish
pocketbook.

My dad, being a bishop, was always wary of scams or fraudulent
products that deceived his flock. One day many years ago, Dad called
my brother Norman and me together for a brief meeting. He told us,

"There are some health products being used that need some investigation." Both Norman and I, being technically inclined, couldn't have been given a better assignment than to do the necessary investigating.

One product was called "The Black Box." This was a diagnosing device that operated very simply: The theory was called *radionics*, a high-tech sounding word for any Amishman. The Black Box had several dials and a well in the center of the box. The sick person placed some human tissue such as hair, blood, or saliva into the well. The practitioner then turned the dials and simultaneously rubbed an adhesive plate. When the adhesive plate became sticky, the health practitioner checked the numbers on his dials. He then consulted a chart which showed him what disease the patient suffered.

The process was so simple and natural that it appealed to the Amish sufferer. The treatment was neither invasive nor expensive when compared to hospitals or medical specialists. It appeared scientific enough to give it credibility, so it surely must be real. In fact, a patient could just send his photograph as a specimen. How convenient! This was, of course, taboo in Amish culture, since photographs are forbidden.

The interesting fact about this particular Black Box was that throughout the years it had lost its technical complexity to the point of having only several wires. In fact, users claimed it worked just as well without batteries installed! The Black Box was definitely suspect.

Our second assignment proved more interesting than the Black Box and very nearly got Dad in trouble.

This particular device was said to detect parasites in the human body and then effectively electrocute them. Upon reading the accompanying literature, one could easily be taken up with the horror of these critters and the necessity to rid oneself of them. Incidentally, Amish parasites are no more pleasant than *English* ones. So now we have these huge promises of health and happiness delivered to eager listeners. Never mind the pocketbook! Never mind the lack of scientific evidence. It looks high-tech and they say it works!

Enter the Amish FBI: Norman and myself.

"Okay," I told Norman, "we can easily duplicate this contraption."

We studied the simple print diagram provided by the author. A resistor here, a transistor there, a condenser between the two, and a speaker to boot. Of course this modern medical device required a battery and even a short copper pipe to hold while it was operated.

With two Amish skeptics bent over the smoking soldering iron and the bishop impatiently waiting for results, the future for Amish parasite hunting was really being threatened. It took a number of intense after-supper sessions in our upstairs bedroom laboratory, but finally we were ready to throw the switch.

The device operated on an interesting theory by detecting certain frequencies radiating from parasites and then sounding a buzz on the speaker. Our ears strained to hear the telltale buzzing sound from the speaker. Nothing. We turned dials up and turned dials down. Nothing. We pulled on this wire. Pushed on that one. Nothing. Surely we weren't that healthy! According to the literature, everyone has parasites!

Giving up was not an option. We had to get answers. So what happens if we add a length of wire to the piece? There! A buzz! And if I take hold of the copper pipe this way, it sounds one way or if that way, it sounds another.

I rushed out of the lab, down the stairs two at a time. I found my father dozing on the rocking chair, but not for long.

"It works!" I yelled.

Dad jumped, his eyes wide. "I don't believe it!" he said, trying to convince himself. His hopes of documenting a hoax caused him to tremble.

"Come and see," I responded.

He followed us upstairs to our detective lab and skeptically eyed our mess of wires.

"Listen," I said, turning the dial while holding the copper pipe. Sure enough, we could hear the *buuzzzzz, buuzzzz.*

There was no mistake. I must have the worms. Dad finally turned and left the lab, thoughtfully stroking his graying beard. Did his boys have parasites, were they practicing witchcraft, or was something else going on?

We decided to take the "something else is going on" road. Norman and I diligently bent to the task before us.

"What if we attach this wire to a longer wire?" was the next logical experiment. The sound changed. It was clearer somehow with less static. Plus, we didn't have to hold the copper pipe any longer. Now we had lots of noise with no human attached. Was the room full of parasites? We didn't think so.

We turned the dial and cranked up the speaker volume.

"Whoa here! I hear voices!" Norman looked shocked.

I planted my ear to the speaker. It was unmistakable. We heard voices. It was unintelligible but distinct, with faint music. Were they parasite voices? Or perhaps spirit voices? Or was something else going on?

By now Dad was worried. What had he gotten his curious boys into? It all started quite innocently but where was this heading? This was certainly no ordinary medical device. But what was it? It certainly seemed like a hoax, but what sort of hoax?

Meanwhile the Amish FBI picked up speed.

"You know, I think this is a crystal radio," I announced after deep contemplation. I compared the two circuits and they were strikingly similar. *The only way to know is to build one,* we concluded innocently enough.

The next day found us at the local electronic shop asking for a diode.

"What do you need a diode for?" the burly proprietor demanded as he riffled through a cardboard box of tiny parts.

My face changed colors as I stuttered, "It's...it's for a project."

I felt foolish but quickly recovered as we hurried home with our precious piece of the puzzle. Once home, it didn't take long to build the crystal radio.

We held our breath, threw the switch, turned the dial and...Presto! It buzzed. And spoke. The same unintelligible garble mixed with faint music. Now we knew. What a hoax! A radio to test for parasites! What a joke. The Amish had spent hundreds of dollars to get tested with nothing better than a radio!

But a week later our tune changed. Dad was worried. His boys had proved that his flock was being fraudulently tested with a helpless hoax. But the troubling part was the only thing the people heard was, "The bishop's boys built a radio!"

Anathema! Radios are worldly! Whoever heard of an Amish bishop letting his boys build a radio?

Fortunately, the truth prevailed and in time Dad proved his sincerity. The project was disassembled and the Amish FBI remained unscathed, none the worse for wear.

Grandfather Eicher

Jerry Eicher

Excerpted from *My Amish Childhood*

> *"Thou shalt rise up before the hoary head, and honour the face of the old man, and fear thy God: I am the* LORD *(Leviticus 19:32).*

THE FAMILY LIVED IN A LONG, WHITE HOUSE WITH LARGE WINDOWS IN the front. Toward the back the house had a wing attached with the mudroom and woodshed. A portion of the house had an upstairs, the roofline leaving the welcoming sweep of the front windows unaffected. Here the sustained memories of that period of childhood lie. I find that strange now. I would have thought they would be at Grandfather Stoll's place, or even at home. But they are not.

Here I remember the prayers at mealtimes around the long table. Grandfather Eicher would lead out in his sing-song chant that charmed and fascinated me. It was as if he knew a secret he wasn't telling us. Some hidden pleasure he had found that we could not yet see.

I remember him laughing. That was how he approached us grandchildren, his white beard flowing down his chest, his face glowing. And it didn't take a special occasion to put him in such a mood. It was as if we were the occasion.

Grandfather Eicher was a minister back then. Once, after we'd returned from living in Honduras with our hearts aching in sorrow, he approached me in the washroom and said there had been complaints that I was singing parts at the Sunday-night hymn singings. He told me, "We don't do things like that around here." He laughed as he said it, and I knew someone had put him up to it. Grandfather Eicher wouldn't have cared one way or the other whether a few bass notes were growled at the hymn singings. But I nodded my agreement. There would be no more parts singing on Sunday nights.

I never knew another man who made you feel so at home, yet he never drew close, as if his heart was always far away, somewhere else.

His preaching is still a distinct memory. When I remember him speaking, I see his face lifted toward the ceiling, his hands clasped in front of him, his white beard flowing over his arms. He could talk a thousand miles an hour, or so it seemed to me. A person could lose himself in that voice. It was as if you were enveloped in love and acceptance. In his preaching he wasn't going anywhere particular. He had no agenda. He simply exalted in holy words, as if he were glad himself to be part of such a great thing.

Grandmother Eicher could chatter during the week about as fast as Grandfather Eicher did on Sundays. She'd say hi, give out a long stream of words, and then bustle on. There was always something going on at the house.

She came from Arthur, Illinois. Grandfather lived in Davies County, Indiana. My guess is they met when he visited Arthur on weekends for weddings or funerals, typical Amish reasons to travel to another town. Grandmother had a great sorrow in life. She'd lost her first love under tragic circumstances before she could marry him. She never forgot that.

The Eicher men worked during the day, either in the fields or on construction jobs, so my visits to Grandfather Eicher's place were always populated with women.

Aunt Rosemary, the youngest aunt on the Eicher side was petite, the prettiest of the sisters. She would end up marrying a rather cultured Amish man from one of the trackless Northern Ontario Amish communities.

Aunt Nancy could move about as fast as Grandfather and Grandmother could talk. She was the shy one, even with us children. She would tilt her head in that peculiar way of hers, as if to deflect some incoming missile. She would marry one of the Stoll cousins, a man who stuttered as I did, although not as severely. Perhaps she had her own sorrows from which her heart reached out to a fellow sufferer.

Aunt Martha was the jolly one, always smiling and happy. I never saw her that she wasn't bubbling with joy. She was also a diabetic from early childhood. I remember she gave herself insulin shots in the leg, and allowed us children to watch. I knew nothing then of the suffer-ings of a diabetic, and still don't, except from secondhand sources. But it could not have been easy for her.

She never married. I don't think I ever heard of a suitor, either. It was just one of those things. Her kidneys gave out in her early fifties, and she soon chose to forgo treatment rather than hire a driver to make the long trips into town. Her decision was influenced perhaps by the expense or simply from the weariness of suffering.

It must have taken great courage to walk so willingly over to the other side. But then I can imagine Aunt Martha facing it with cheer-ful acceptance. I suppose she was welcomed home with more joy than many of the earth's great ones. I know she lived close to the Father's heart.

Though most of my childhood I grew up in Honduras surrounded by the vigorous intellectual life of the Stoll relatives, it was from here, at Grandfather Eicher's home, that I draw the characters of my Amish fic-tion. The white walls, the long dinner table, the open living room, the small, spotless bathrooms, the yard outside with its swing tied high in the tree. And above all from the feeling of simple living. These people profess to be nobody special. There's a minister in the house, and later a bishop, but you wouldn't know it. They simply laughed a lot.

I've not always lived like that. Being honest, I've hardly ever lived like that. Life has been a hard climb, and each peak only reveals another. In those moments when I come home, this is where I come to. To Grandfather Eicher's house. I shouldn't be surprised, but I am.

Working with the Threshing Ring

Philip Stoll

*And your threshing shall reach unto the vintage, and the vintage
shall reach unto the sowing time: and ye shall eat your bread
to the full, and dwell in your land safely (Leviticus 26:5).*

LIFE ON OUR FARM WAS GOOD. THERE WERE ALWAYS ENOUGH THINGS
going on that changed with the seasons to keep things lively. And today
was threshing day at Uncle Joe's place right across from us. We quickly
finished breakfast as I wanted to arrive first and begin to spread out the
shocks so they could dry in the morning sunshine. That was always fun.

Today I'd be one of the pitchers. This was a job I really enjoyed.
We'd all work together as a team and see how many wagonloads we
could get in for the day. Our team of trusty Percherons, Bird and Babe,
would stay home as they'd be needed here on the farm. There would be
plenty of others who would arrive at Uncle Joe's place with their wagons and horses.

I'd still harness Bird and Babe, I figured. They'd come in with
the cows earlier, and this was a job I loved. So much so that my parents teased me about it. They said my name Philip, "lover of horses,"
couldn't have been more fitting. That was me.

Bird and Babe were a hardworking and safe team. They were a
delight for my younger siblings to drive. So now I quickly grabbed
Bird's collar and slipped it over her head, then did the same for Babe's.
I made sure the mares' necks were rubbed down and had no soft puffs
or sores. Dad had taught me how to wash their shoulders with warm
salt water. That way there was little chance they'd ever get collar sores.

"The righteous man," Dad told us often, quoting Proverbs 12:10,
"regardeth the life of his beast."

After harnessing the horses I hitched them to our wagon parked in front of the house. I knew Bird and Babe would wait there patiently until they were needed by my siblings. So out the lane I went in my bare feet with my pitchfork in hand.

At Uncle Joe's place I was greeted by another neighbor and friend, Jacob Reimer. He was younger than me, but we had grown close as friends. I was delighted to head to the fields with him. There we began to spread out the sheaves. We only did this until we had enough for the morning's work. By the afternoon the shocks would have dried all the way through.

Setting up the shocks earlier in the season had also been a rewarding time. We used 11 sheaves and began with a bundle in the middle with four more set around that. This was all done at a slight angle so they placed equal pressure on the center. We followed this with four more on the sides and two for the roof. We fanned out the ones on top to shed most of the rain. An additional value from a shock like this is that enzymes are added to the grain. It's little wonder that with the coming of the combine and modern farming practices our health is on the decline.

As Jacob and I worked, we speculated who would show up first with a wagon so we could begin to load. Our attention was soon distracted when we discovered a skunk had taken up residence in a corn shock along Catfish Creek. Ever so politely we gave Mr. Skunk the freedom to decide when the appropriate time was for him to wander off on his merry way. In the meantime, we took up work in a different area.

Moments later there was the distant rumble of an approaching wagon. *Surely it has to be Uncle Mark, for he drives like Jehu of old,* I thought. And presently a Belgian team galloped down the road, proving me correct. Uncle Mark soon arrived and tied his team of steeds then strode across the field at a fast pace.

"Good morning," he said, full of cheer as he began to help us.

There's nothing lazy or laid-back about this uncle of mine, and we looked forward to loading his wagon. There's also never a dull moment or a slow one with Uncle Mark. He's the one who sees humor in our desperation to keep up with the sheaves that he sends flying in from every angle while he loads the wagon.

We soon began and several wagonloads later, the hot sun drove Jacob and me to seek a refreshing drink of water served in the shade of a giant maple. But then here came Uncle Mark again, hollering for us to come out of the shade and load another wagon. After another quick swallow we joined him, and the sheaves flew again. Uncle Mark was on the wagon this time. We were determined to cover him up. But as quickly as we threw the sheaves up, just as quickly he had them spread.

I whispered to Jacob, "Hey, let's both jab into this standing shock and heave all eleven up at once."

So with a great grunt we managed the feat, then rushed to add more sheaves before Uncle Mark could recover.

"Boys!" he hollered. "Slow down." Which was just the reward we wanted.

We laughed as we relished the fact we could, with a united effort, bog him down.

By lunchtime we were tired and scrambled on an empty wagon for the trip to the house where we washed up. Aunt Laura and her girls had prepared mashed potatoes, gravy, corn, and potato salad for lunch. But best of all were the chocolate whoopee pies and homemade ice cream with chocolate topping for dessert. We all ate heartily, and afterward took a short rest out on the lawn.

When we went back to work, I was assigned the horrible task of spreading the straw in the loft. This is a very dirty job with lots of dust. But also a job that needed to be done. So I looked forward to the afternoon break when I could come down and get a nice, refreshing breeze blowing in my face. All the while we enjoyed cold watermelon and more chocolate whoopee pies.

Then, oh wonder of wonders, I got to go out to the fields again.

Later, when chore time rolled around, our crew got smaller, but we renewed our efforts. Our goal was to complete another small field that day at yet another farm, with all the straw in the mow and the fields ready to grow a lush stand of hay that had been seeded with the oat sheaves.

As the sun began to sink we loaded the last of the oats and stared down the road to the threshing machine. Our hearts were gladdened with yet another job well done, our goal accomplished. When we work together like this, what great rewards can be gleaned. Truly the joy of sharing and loving each other above ourselves is a wonderful, rewarding life lived for the Lord.

My Scary Day of Silo Filling

Philip Stoll

And even to your old age I am he; and even to hoar hairs
will I carry you: I have made, and I will bear; even I
will carry, and will deliver you (Isaiah 46:4).

DAYLIGHT FAST APPROACHED AS THE STOLL FAMILY DESERTED THEIR comfortable beds to begin a new day. At 4:30 a.m. it was high time to be in the barn and get the milking under way. With more than 70 goats to milk by hand, feed, and water (plus milk for the goat kids), there was a great need that we all work together.

Dad often was heard to say, "Early to bed, early to rise, makes a man healthy, wealthy, and wise."

This proverb has been impressed upon each of us from an early age. So as the morning progressed we hurried about. I quickly gave the milking does their hay and then checked for any new babies born overnight. Lo and behold, I found a doe with babies all around her. I kept counting and found it hard to grasp when the number came to seven. We had never had more than quadruplets before. So I got busy and made sure all of them had been able to eat breakfast. While I did this, the news spread rapidly of this unusual occurrence, and several of my siblings gathered.

Meanwhile, the chores continued. The milking hadn't stopped, and Dad was taking care of our one family cow. There were also calves to be fed and the chickens tended to. For all this activity, we only had the main kerosene pressure lantern and two small hurricane lamps. But we made do. Gideon, my oldest brother, helped me harness a team of our horses, Queen and Black Beauty. Black Beauty was high-spirited most of the time and Gideon wasn't too fond of her, so he took Queen.

Talking gently and soothingly I set to work on getting Black Beauty's harness on.

When we finished, we all headed for the house where Mom's wholesome breakfast awaited us. This morning Mom had biscuits and hamburger gravy waiting with grapefruit and fresh whole milk. After we ate, we gathered in the living room for devotions. Dad read a chapter and expounded on the Scripture. We sang two songs after that. Kneeling for prayer, Dad earnestly asked for all his children's safety, and also for the missionaries working in other lands. Little did we realize what the day was to hold for me, or the power of prayer.

With devotions finished, my siblings still in school hurried out the door for the schoolhouse up the road. I ran out to the barn to hitch Queen and Black Beauty to the wagon and be on my way. I planned to help two of our neighborhood newlywed couples for the day—Wayne and Roseanna and Harold and Lillian. Both young families lived on the 80-acre farm behind us.

I drove our frisky horses down their long lane. As I crossed the culvert I eyed every inch of the creek line to see if I might spot muskrats. I was anxious to run my own traps once the pelts were prime. The field southwest of the lane and along Catfish Creek was where we would be getting our corn to fill the silo today. I figured if we worked hard maybe we could finish. The air was quite fresh this morning, and with no frost on the ground we could begin work sooner.

Harold had been my seventh and eighth grade teacher. He was also my first cousin and a close friend. Now he came out of the barn with his team of three horses and we headed into the field where the binder sat. After a cheery greeting, we hitched his horses to the binder and with the arrival of Nathaniel, Harold's youngest brother, we were ready to begin.

With Harold on the binder, I drove the team on the wagon alongside the loader. Nathaniel stood ready to stack the bundles as they arrived. There's always a feeling of accomplishment as one keeps the wagon team at just the right spot under the loader in order to give the fellow on the wagon the least amount of work. I exalted in the joy of the job as the morning sunshine basked us with its early rays. The corn was still dew-drenched and the smells were fresh. We traveled up and down the long rows of standing corn. When the wagon was nearly loaded, we cheered at the sight of Harold's brother David arriving with another wagon and team to help us. We finished Nathaniel's load, and I jumped off to climb on David's wagon. I greeted him heartily and asked, "Do you want to load or try your hand at driving?"

"Why don't you drive?" David answered. "I'll load to warm up from the chilly drive over here."

So I drove alongside the binder and the next wagon started to fill. This team wasn't as spirited. I had my hands full urging them to keep an appropriate speed. I also didn't want to work David harder than necessary by being in the wrong place with the wagon. As we rounded the back side of the field, two more of our crew arrived, twin brothers Daniel and James, and we were complete for the day.

We rotated after a few loads and I loaded a wagon for a change. When we unloaded at the silage cutter, Harold made sure I knew that if the bundles got stuck, under no circumstance was I to jump on the web to get the corn unstuck. He warned me that if I fell and the plug began to move I could end up getting badly hurt and even killed.

But all went well on the load. We only had one partial plug. I dutifully jumped off the wagon and got it started from the ground. Afterward I headed back to the field for another load. All of this was done with no mishaps. Normal and safe started to become routine.

But as the day wore on, I grew more weary. Perhaps that's why I lost my good sense and became careless. Because when I got another plug, I ignored Harold's earlier warning and lightly jumped on the web and then back off again to unplug it. This way I knew I wouldn't lose any time. I threw on the bundles at a reckless pace and everything seemed fine. I thought I had stumbled on an efficient way to unplug the bundles without having to jump to the ground each time.

Soon I got even bolder and in so doing, I lost my balance on the web and fell forward headfirst, headed right for the cutters. The fright I felt was awful, and I could think of no way to get off in time, until I thought of the overhead safety bar situated above the twirling blades.

I threw up my hands, and oh joy, the web hit reverse and emptied me and the bundles on the cement under the wagon. I lay there for a moment in shock. Finally I jumped up and put the web in forward again. I was afraid the others in the field would have heard the tractor rev and ask what had happened. But they kept on working, and I headed out to the field.

Once I arrived, James looked me over and announced that I looked tired. "Time to drive the team again," he said. I was just grateful he didn't ask what had happened to me.

After lunch I took a turn at packing down the silage and was unprepared for Harold's pointed question. "I thought the cutter ran empty longer than normal this forenoon when you were unloading. Did something go wrong?"

Looking at the ground, I replied, "Yes. I started to jump on the web to unplug it, since that seemed much faster. But I ended up falling headfirst on the web. I only reversed it just in time."

I glanced at Harold and noticed he was quite pale.

"Philip," he said, "God still has something important for you to do. He spared you when you were within inches of being chopped up. How awful I would have felt for being responsible for your death. I trust you won't do that ever again."

Harold had a fair amount of dampness around his eyes as he spoke. And I was a much chided boy with a lot to think about. The greatness of God's mercy in saving my life swept over me. The day seemed brighter, clearer, and warmer. I even sang as sometime later the wagon bumped back out to the field. It all seemed like a fitting response that day, and God has given me the desire to serve Him faithfully wherever He may call.

Babies Don't Wear Watches

Esther Weaver

*But thou art he that took me out of the womb: thou didst make
me hope when I was upon my mother's breasts (Psalm 22:9).*

It's 1:50 a.m. I slowly wake up to my husband's deep breathing beside me. Bright headlights stream through the slatted blinds. Is that a car going by, or is it someone pulling in the driveway? No, I decide optimistically, surely it's only a car passing by. Seconds later, my heart rate hits the roof. Beep! Beep! Beep! Three shrill blasts from a car horn rip the night air. This sounds all too familiar. But why tonight? Why must new babies come in the middle of the night?

Six weeks ago my mother-in-law, Ella Weaver, who is also a midwife, underwent major hip surgery. Her recovery has been fantastic, but she still doesn't have her full strength back, so she needs occasional assistance with the births. Daisy, Ella's youngest daughter, and I offered to help Ella when she needs us. And most of the babies we've helped with were born during the night. So either the babies don't know how to tell time, or they just don't care how much they inconvenience us. Of course I'm beginning to believe the latter. Could this be the reason my peaceful night is being so rudely interrupted?

"Honey," I call gently, hoping my voice will somehow penetrate my husband's sleep-addled brain, "Someone's here!"

"Wha…oh…uh…," he mumbles as he stiffly lumbers out of bed.

I dizzily race around the room trying to decide what to wear. I settle for a comfortable as well as practical blue dress, yank it over my head, and follow my hubby in his hasty tumble out of the bedroom.

In the meantime, Daisy has somehow managed to find her way inside our house, even though most of our doors are locked. She mumbles, "Oh, you're already up."

"What's happening?" I ask, although I already know.

"A mother from Jonesville is in labor. Ella's waiting in the car."

"Okay." I continue my dressing and pull my hair into a lopsided bun. I hastily pin on my covering.

I run out to the kitchen where my faithful husband is getting my purse ready. He's stuffing it with all the essentials: snacks, money, a water bottle, and my headlamp. The lighting system in some Amish houses is slightly lacking so it's always best to be prepared.

"Thank you so much, honey." I sigh gratefully as I swing the purse over my shoulder. I tell him goodbye and wish him a good rest of the night. I dash out to the waiting vehicle, jump inside, and slide the door shut.

I glance over at Daisy, who's trying to catch a few winks of sleep on the seat beside me.

Mrs. Carol Cousineau, our chauffeur for the trip, carefully wheels out of our driveway and onto the quiet road. I chat a few minutes with Ella, who's in the front seat, before I settle down for a snooze on the 45-minute drive.

Unfortunately, we aren't the only creatures up at this insane hour. Carol brakes suddenly and violently, throwing us forward and narrowly avoiding three deer. Bambi blinks at us and trots off unhurriedly. We cautiously roll on with Carol on guard for more daring creatures.

As we wheel through the town of Jonesville, our GPS blinks and loses its satellite reception. "You can't do that on us," gasps Carol. "What was the next road?"

A few seconds later, it wakes up again and faithfully guides us on. Carol and Ella sigh with relief. Maybe the satellites are also wondering why we're waking them at this hour.

I relax and vainly wish I knew the roads and had a better sense of direction. Five minutes later the GPS directs a right turn in half a mile. We obediently turn right at the next crossroad only to be rebuffed by the GPS's flat, nasal, "Recalculating."

"What did I do wrong?" Carol questions in a concerned voice.

"I think we're all right. Just keep going," Ella assures us.

"But it says *recalculating*. I must have made a wrong turn," insists Carol.

"I wasn't paying attention," I apologize from the backseat. "But there was no place else to turn."

Thus reassured we drive on. A few uneventful miles later, we arrive at the address and pull into the driveway of a large, well-kept farm.

It is precisely 3:00 a.m. All of us except Carol pile out. Ella hurries inside the dimly lit house to assess the situation while Daisy and I grab all of the birthing paraphernalia from the trunk and waddle toward the house with our arms overflowing. We manage to safely deposit all the gear on the kitchen floor without losing our balance among the shadows.

Ella reenters the kitchen from the even more dimly lit bedroom and tells us the baby should come soon. We hope. I run out to converse with Carol. I feel bad that she has to wait. "I guess you have an agreement with Ella to hang around," I state more than ask. "Would you like a bed to lie down?"

"No," she says. "I'll stay out here until I get cold and then I'll come in."

"Okay. That's fine," I say, and hurry back to the house. Inside we start digging through the bags, getting everything ready, while the young farmer and father-to-be thoughtfully lights a bright gas lamp. First, we get all the baby things out on the kitchen table—the scales, tape measure, blue and pink inkpads to take the baby's footprints, a waterproof pad, and an old but clean blanket to wrap the baby. Daisy digs out the mother's birth records and starts recording information. I dig out the birthing tub, lay it out on the living room floor, and start laboriously inflating it, using a hand pump. Daisy takes her turn, cheerfully commenting on the hopeful possibility of us developing strong, lean back muscles from all this exercise.

The young farmer steps out of the bedroom carrying his first-born 14-month-old daughter and takes her across the yard to Grandma's house. When he returns, he takes over the slow tub inflation process. We gratefully turn it over to his much stronger arms and back. After he's done, he fills it with warm water. His wife by this time is in active labor, and ready for the much more spacious birthing tub. We help her get in and try to make her as comfortable as possible, although any mother knows that *comfortable* is not the right word to describe any part of the birthing process.

We fan her flushed and sweating face, let her squeeze our hands, put a cool cloth on her forehead, verbally encourage her, and try to keep her focused.

Finally, after two more hours of hard, painful labor, she gives birth to a handsome, kicking, and screaming little son. We all sigh with thankfulness and relief. Daisy takes the baby, bathes, weighs, and measures him, and dresses him in clean, soft baby clothes. The young farmer helps Ella and me lift the weary mother out of the tub and situate her comfortably in bed. We slowly drain and deflate the tub and pack up our gear. We are almost ready to leave when the shrill ringtones of Ella's pager penetrates our weary minds. "Oh, no!" we sigh. "Not another baby!"

Ella goes to call at the nearest phone and confirms our fears. Daisy and I, though, will not travel to this one. Thankfully there are enough grandmas there that they don't need our help. We sigh in sheer relief.

Faithful Carol has managed to sneak a couple winks of sleep and drives us home without event. Once there, Daisy and I hit our comfortable pillows and conk out. No more ringtones—for a little while anyway.

Nearing the Dawn
Laura Yoder

But if any widow have children or nephews, let them learn
first to show piety at home, and to requite their parents: for
that is good and acceptable before God (1 Timothy 5:4).

DAD AND MOM HAVE GONE TO ALBERT AND ADA MARIE'S WEDDING.
The couple is older than the usual marrying age. Albert has been a
widower for some time. As I thought of Dad and Mom driving to
Albert's wedding, my memories returned to the past, to Albert's first
wife, Rosanna. I can remember playing dolls with Rosanna when we
were girls. We used to climb trees together and talk of our grown-up
years lying ahead of us. I remember I was eight years old the day we solemnly promised each other we would be friends forever.

Then we both grew up and married. She soon moved away to a
neighboring community and then later the news of her cancer came
as a shock. Rosanna was 38 with five young children when she died. I
was standing on my sister's porch when the news arrived. The rest of
the day is lost to my memory, but that moment remains, standing there
on the porch with the sun shining and the wind whipping my skirts.

Albert was a widower for over a year, which wasn't easy with five
children, I'm sure. He is marrying Rosanna's older sister, a bittersweet
time, which Dad and Mom have been invited to share.

With my parents gone to the wedding, someone needs to care for
Grandma. Grandma's mind is almost gone, although she has lived a full
and happy life. Grandma married Grandpa in Ohio, and they moved
to Indiana while their children were still young. After Grandpa passed
away, she lived alone until her failing health caught up with her. Mom
is her only daughter, and moving here to Michigan from her settled
place in Indiana where her roots were deep wasn't easy. But Grandma

has come to feel at home here. Though she misses the family in Indiana, when she went back to visit, she missed the family here too.

In the days when Grandma's mind was clear, I enjoyed visiting with her. She'd talk of days gone by, of the little sister Mom never knew, who died a few hours after she was born. Grandma remembered the tragic things in life—the boy in the community who passed when he was four, the time my uncle lost his foot in a farm accident.

Then Grandma would smile as her thoughts turned to better times. One of her favorite things, she told us, was going on a buggy ride in a slow rain.

"It seems like such a little thing," Grandma said. "But it remains one of my favorite memories."

I could picture that buggy ride in the slow rain quite well. I could see Grandpa and Grandma going down the road with their faithful driving horse, Darkie, the rain drizzling against the storm front, running in rivulets down the glass.

But those years are gone now. Grandma is 94 and nearly helpless. Someone has to stay with her all the time, so my sisters and I have volunteered. There are six of us, but two live out of state, and my oldest sister, Ruth Ann, has back problems, so that leaves three of us to stay with Grandma today.

Martha, my youngest sister, is married to Jacob Byler. She will arrive early to help with Grandma. She has two small children who still aren't in school. Katie and I have children to see off, so Martha will be at Dad and Mom's place to get Grandma out of bed.

My morning also began early on the farm. With seven children it's always busy. We were out of bed at 4:30 to begin the milking. There are 25 cows needing tending to. Afterward my husband, Mark, and our older children, Alan, Sarah, and Mahlon, finished the feeding and bedding. I cleaned the milk house.

Sun rays were lighting the sky in the east by the time I hurried to the house. First, there were the rest of the children to get up: Senesa, Elmina, Melvin, and Eunice. The younger ones need help getting dressed before breakfast is begun and the school lunches packed. In the meantime the other children come in from the barn. There are now four schoolchildren hustling about, getting washed up, changing from chore clothing into school clothes, putting on shoes. There's never enough of me to reach around in the morning.

When things settle down, breakfast is a quiet interlude with everyone filling up on eggs, toast, and cereal. A couple hours of chores outside in the cold makes for empty stomachs and a good appetite. After breakfast the pace picks up again as the schoolchildren dash about, gathering up books, lunches, coats, and mittens. Usually there are at least one or two lost items to search for. Finally, with cheery goodbyes, they rush out the door, and the house settles into silence. I have time to think about my planned visit to Grandma today.

Usually I sit and relax for a few minutes at this point, but I know Martha needs help so I keep going. Katie would no doubt arrive before me at Dad and Mom's place, since she doesn't have a farm and only three children. And I am right. Katie's buggy is there when I arrive. Martha and Katie have finished Grandma's morning sponge bath and taken care of the open sore on her back. They dressed Grandma and placed her in the wheelchair. Even with the two of them, they had found this quite a job, they told me. But Grandma is now eating breakfast.

Mom had shown me how to soak and dress the sores on Grandma's feet. Grandma is a diabetic, so sores are a constant concern and hard to heal. With Grandma's breakfast finished, I tackle the job. I prepare two bowls of water, one hot and the other cold. I begin by soaking Grandma's feet—four minutes in the hot and half a minute in the cold. Back and forth, back and forth.

Grandma's a patient soul and seldom complains. Frequently she doesn't recognize us and will talk about people and things the rest of us can't see. Today she hasn't recognized my sisters, but she now knows who I am and she's patient with my inexperience.

When the soaking is done, it's time to clean the sores. This one especially is bad. I hand over the task to Katie for a moment, stepping outside in the fresh air. I'm soon able to go on, and the two of us rebandage the foot with burdock leaves and salve.

With everything completed, we give Grandma her pills and settle her back into her wheelchair. Things are as comfortable for Grandma as we can make it. Katie and I sit down and look at each other. It's nearly lunchtime. We have been busy most of the forenoon taking care of Grandma—all three of us.

I think for the first time we realize everything Mom does. It's only in the last months that Grandma has become so helpless. We had been trying to stop by and help. But even with the best efforts of us sisters and sisters-in-law, the bulk of the work falls to Mom.

We soon make lunch and eat. It's later in the afternoon when we help Grandma with her first bathroom trip. She tells us in her soft, quivery voice, "Ach...I never dreamed I would come to this."

Tears prick my eyes as I tell her, "We're glad to do this for you. Someday it might be one of us."

I tried to imagine how that would be. I know it can't be easy, becoming ever more helpless and suffering these indignities. My mind went back through the years to when Grandpa was still alive. That was 25 years ago. He also wasn't well before he passed away. I remember Grandma helping Grandpa with the same things we were now helping her with. During his last weeks, we had visited them. I sat beside Grandpa at the table and his hands trembled when I passed the dishes to him. Once he dropped a dish and Grandma reached over and steadied it for him.

Grandpa had been a farmer. He knew about long, full days of working in the fields. His last days contained none of that, though. His body succumbed to Parkinson's. His feet shuffled. His hands shook. His voice was weak. Grandpa was bedridden the last month. I was only 13.

Now Grandma is where Grandpa had been. The years keep marching by, and if time continues for us, we too might someday come to this place. It's a sobering thought.

At the end of the day, we go home with a greater empathy, not only for Grandma and Mom, but for all the elderly who must give up everything they've been used to. Bit by bit, they lose out. We pray they will have faithful caregivers.

Life begins for us when we are young. We grow up and see the same thing happen with our own children. We diaper and bathe our babies.

We dress and feed them. We do it year after year with each new arrival. There are sacrifices and it's a lot of work, but it's a joyful calling full of rewards and filled with promise and expectation. With training and prayer we expect our children to grow up and live a life of service.

It is different when we reach the other end and our life of service is over. The mind and body are ebbing. There's a beauty that comes with the acceptance of this, as there is in the devoted services of the caregiver, though both are tinged with sadness. We consider caring for Grandma a priceless privilege, and one which places our own lives in a clearer perspective. We do it gladly, knowing God has a purpose and a plan, and it is good.

New Beginnings

Nathan Miller

Excerpted from *Out of Deception*

*For by grace are ye saved through faith; and that not
of yourselves: it is the gift of God: Not of works, lest
any man should boast (Ephesians 2:8-9).*

I TURNED INTO MY BROTHER ALVA'S DRIVEWAY WITH APPREHENSION IN
my heart. What would my new life in Evart be like? It had been hard to
leave what I knew…but after having broken free from what was a cult-
like experience with self-proclaimed prophet Wilbur Lee, I was ready
to move on. Hopefully it would be here in Evart.

Alva's wife, Elnora, gave me a warm welcome—hopefully that was
a sign of good things to come. I carried my luggage in the house and
got everything situated in my room. Soon Alva came home from work
for lunch. After he welcomed me and showed me around the place, we
went inside to eat.

Throughout the next several days, Alva and I had many long discussions about my life with Wilbur Lee. Freely sharing my experi-
ences allowed me to view them from a completely different perspective.
Many times I was embarrassed to relate what we had believed as a
group.

On Sunday, church services were held at Alva's house. I sat in rapt
attention as the ministers expounded God's Word. I felt like a dry
sponge soaking up the living water of truth.

"Jesus was here as a human being, yet He was without sin," the minister preached. "His purpose was to bring hope to lost mankind. He is
the great healer of our souls. One of His missions on earth was to bring
physical healing. This was God's way of getting people to believe Him.

He healed a number of lepers. Leprosy was a terminal illness, yet He healed them every time."

Wilbur Lee had never healed anyone. He could not even heal Mary's cancer. Suddenly I remembered the vision of Jesus I had had after leaving Wilbur Lee's. I hadn't thought about it for months. I began to think maybe Jesus was the Son of God after all. The minister certainly seemed confident that what he was preaching was the truth. And he didn't spend time knocking other churches; he simply presented the Bible.

"The Bible is absolutely true," the minister continued. "How do we know it is true? First of all because of the difference it makes in our lives when we believe its truths and live them. Jesus tells us in His Word what we are to do."

My mind flashed back to my vision. *Oh, so that's what Jesus meant when He told me, "Do as I say."* Perhaps if I had searched the Bible and believed everything it said, things would have turned out differently. Instead, my life was sure a mess now. I needed to find the truth.

After church the bishop walked up to me. "So you are Alva's brother?"

"Yes, I am," I responded.

"My name is Omer Miller. I'm glad to see you here. You're welcome to come to our house to visit anytime," he said.

That evening Alva and I sat in the living room visiting. My thoughts returned to the sermon.

"Alva, how do you know the Bible is true?" I asked.

"I simply believe it is true," he stated with confidence. "It has made all the difference in my life."

"When I left Wilbur Lee the first time, I read the first chapter of Romans. I could really identify with that."

"That's what you need to do. You have to read the Bible. The more you read it, the clearer it will become," he advised. "All the answers to our troubles are in there."

"So, you don't believe it makes one proud to read the Bible too much?" I asked.

Alva chuckled. "No, certainly not. If we read it for the right reasons, it will humble us. It shows us how sinful we are before God and how helpless we are without Him."

"Why would God kill His Son, Jesus, if He is a God of love?" I asked.

"God didn't kill Him. The angry people killed Him. However, God allowed Him to die because there was no other way for us humans to be saved from our sins. Ever since Adam and Eve sinned, blood was required to redeem the sinner from his condemnation. God is righteous; therefore, He cannot tolerate any sin. All of us have sinned at some time in our life. In the Old Testament the priest would offer an animal's blood as atonement, which worked for a time, but God wanted to cleanse us from our sins for all time. Animals were not sufficient to take away our sins.

"The only person who qualified was Jesus, because He never committed a sin. He was completely pure and innocent. He became our prophet, priest, and king. God sent Jesus down to earth in the form of a baby, and when He grew to manhood, He endured all the temptations that we have, yet He did not commit sin. God knew that nobody is good enough by his own strength to please Him and enter heaven; therefore, God allowed the people to kill Him. However, He did not leave Him in the grave. Three days later Jesus rose from death. Now He lives at the right hand of God in heaven. If we confess our sins, believe Him with our whole heart, accept Him in our lives, and repent, or turn away from our sins, then He will give us His Holy Spirit and we can have victory over sin. Isn't that wonderful?"

I was spellbound. I had never heard anything like this. "It seems like Wilbur Lee may have taught something like this in the beginning, but it sure didn't last long," I said.

"When Jesus saves us from our sins, He also forgives us for all the bad things we have ever done. We don't have to live with a guilty conscience anymore. However, when we accept Jesus as our Savior, we must also accept Him as our Lord. We do what He tells us in His Word, the Bible. If we disobey Him, we become guilty again. We must confess our sins; then He will forgive us and we become clean again. The only sin that cannot be forgiven is the sin that isn't repented of," Alva said.

"But what if we commit the unpardonable sin of blasphemy of the Holy Ghost?" I asked.

"Well," Alva responded, "God convicts us through the Holy Spirit. As long as we are resisting and speaking against the Holy Spirit, there is no forgiveness. When we choose to listen to His promptings and respond, He will forgive us. A person who is concerned about having committed an unpardonable sin can rest assured that he has not. If you are concerned, that's a sign that the Holy Spirit is working in your life. If He is convicting you, He hasn't left you. The Holy Spirit is faithful to convict you. He will come repeatedly, attempting to get your attention. If you resist Him too long, there will be a point when He comes for the last time. We do not know for certain when that time is. We do know one can never repent and be forgiven after death. In 1 John 1:9, it says, 'If we confess our sins, He is faithful and just to forgive us our sins, and to cleanse us from all unrighteousness.'"

"That sure sounds more hopeful than what I have been taught so far!" I exclaimed. "Wilbur Lee taught us that becoming angry is a sign that we have blasphemed the Holy Ghost. And yet, he became angry himself."

Alva chuckled, "Well, according to his own teachings, Wilbur Lee must have committed the unpardonable sin."

Two evenings later I went to Bishop Omer's house to visit. He invited me inside and we made ourselves comfortable in the living room.

"So, what did you and your group believe?" he asked me.

"The group we were involved with is a cult," I began.

"It's interesting that there would be a cult consisting only of Amish," Omer said skeptically. "Why would you join a cult?"

"That's hard to explain. We were searching for meaning in life. Wilbur Lee took an interest in us and gave answers to many of our questions," I said. "In the beginning he taught us from the Bible, but after a while he developed his own teachings and taught us revelations he supposedly received from the Father."

"After he had lured you away from the Amish church?" he asked.

"Yes. Once we lost faith in the things we'd been taught and those who had taught us, we were vulnerable. Now I don't even have Wilbur Lee. I guess I'm on my own."

"Do you have any plans for your future?" he asked.

"Well, I'm sure I don't want to be Amish," I chuckled nervously.

"I see. What is your impression of the Amish?" Omer asked.

"Not very good," I responded. "Most of them are hypocrites who don't know what they believe. They allow smoking, drinking, dirty jokes, and sins like that in the church and don't do anything about it. They just live the way they do because that's the way their ancestors lived."

"Unfortunately, there are Amish churches that allow sin in the church," the bishop said. "You will find a large variation amongst the Amish as far as what they allow and how they apply the Scriptures. But many Amish churches do not allow sin. The Amish lifestyle doesn't save us. Perhaps too many Amish do believe that way, but it's not scriptural. We believe that we have eternal life by trusting Jesus for our redemption."

"So you don't think I would be saved just by joining the Amish?" I questioned.

"Certainly not," Omer answered. "We believe that Jesus Christ is the only way to eternal life."

"I've often wondered what actually is sinful about electricity or driving cars."

"True, we don't use certain modern conveniences, but that's only for our safety, not our salvation. We believe that living a simple lifestyle brings fewer distractions to our spiritual life."

"I see. I've never heard that explanation before," I said.

Omer continued, "It's important to understand that while these things are not evil in themselves, we as a church do see a danger in them, so we made guidelines accordingly."

"I don't fully understand," I responded. "But I do know that when I decided to throw out all religion and do as I pleased, my life went to shambles."

"Did you ever have any personal encounters with God?" Omer asked.

"Yes, actually I did," I replied. "The night before I left Wilbur Lee I experienced a vision of myself kneeling in front of Jesus." I related my experience in detail. "Am I saved by that experience?"

"No, I wouldn't feel that you are saved from your sins because of that experience since there was no repentance," Omer said. "But God was certainly showing you His love and showing you a way out."

"So what must I do to be saved?" I asked.

"You must first see the sinfulness of your heart and see that you are lost without Jesus in your life. Once you realize your sinfulness, you must come to God, confess your sins, give Jesus your whole heart, and allow Him to be your Master. Jesus will cleanse your heart, forgive your sins, and fill your heart with peace. You need to trust Jesus with your whole life and be willing to follow in loving obedience. Once saved, you can rest assured you will meet Him in heaven if you remain in complete submission to Him. It is important that you realize that we are saved through His gift of grace and not by any works we have done."

I nodded soberly as I rose to leave. *This makes more sense than anything Wilbur Lee ever taught,* I thought.

I spent the next several months studying the Bible and trying to sort out the false doctrines I had been taught. It was a time of intense reflection and coming to grips with the sinfulness of my own heart. Finally, one evening as I was giving the horses their hay, I was seriously contemplating the lost condition of my heart and the great emptiness that was still not satisfied. The burden of my heart was more than I could bear, and I became desperate to find peace. I knelt beside the hay manger, spread out my arms in front of me, and cried out to God.

"O God, You know how sinful I am. I'm sorry for all the sins I've committed in my life. I feel so dirty. I'm sorry for the times that I lied. I am sorry for hating Wilbur Lee. I am sorry for my immorality and pride. I ask You to be my Lord and Savior. Amen."

Indescribable peace enveloped my heart. Tears filled my eyes as I realized that I was delivered from Satan and his lies. Now I was a child of God. Reverently I bowed my head and whispered, "Thank You, God, for saving my soul and forgiving all my sins."

I stood up and walked out of that barn with a light heart. I was a new creature in Christ. My heart overflowed with praise and thankfulness to my Savior for the redeeming grace and love He showed me by cleansing my heart and filling my emptiness with His peace.

Goodbye, Grandma

Joanna Yoder

He that dwelleth in the secret place of the most High shall
abide under the shadow of the Almighty (Psalm 91:1).

I GAZED RESTLESSLY OUT OF THE VAN WINDOW AT THE HILLS OF PENN-sylvania. Since 7:00 that morning we had been traveling from our Michigan home. Finally, after eight hours, we were almost to Grand-pa's house. We had come for a cousin's wedding tomorrow, but more importantly we wanted to see Grandma.

For three years Grandma had been fighting cancer. Chemother-apy had helped keep the disease at bay, but slowly her body had grown weaker. It was clear to Grandpa and the doctors that she couldn't last much longer.

Our driver turned into Grandpa's driveway and we all climbed out to stretch our stiff legs. Aunt Wilma opened the front door and invited us into Grandpa's cozy house. Mom greeted Aunt Wilma with a hug while Dad asked, "How's Grandma?"

"She's sleeping a lot today," Aunt Wilma answered. "But you can go on in and talk with her."

One by one we stepped up to the hospital bed set up beside the liv-ing room window.

When I saw Grandma, my stomach lurched. She was so thin!

"Hi, Grandma," I spoke earnestly and grasped her hand.

"Hi, Joanna." Her lips moved in a weak whisper.

"We're praying for you," I said.

"Thank you."

I could barely hear her answer. Grandma's eyes closed wearily. For a moment I gazed at her thin form and her sunken eyes. I turned away, overcome by a sudden wave of nausea. This was not the grandma I remembered.

We soon left for the evening to stay at another relative's place. We stopped in again two days later when the wedding was over. Grandpa was sitting in his recliner and didn't get up to greet us. His body was crippled with Parkinson's disease, but I marveled at how good he looked. His handshake was still strong.

"Grandpa, we're praying for you," I told him. "I'm sure this isn't easy for you."

"Keep on praying," Grandpa replied with a tear in his eye.

Grandma seemed a little better this morning. She was awake and alert, yet we knew this could be our final goodbye to her. She hadn't eaten in four days and could hardly swallow liquids.

Grandma had always loved to talk, but now the chemo had ruined her voice.

"Oh, if only I could talk," she whispered as one by one we bade her farewell.

When it was my turn, I bent down and placed my hand on her bony shoulder and whispered, "Goodbye, Grandma."

"Goodbye, Joanna," she replied softly.

I tried desperately to think of the right words. "Grandma, go to Jesus and wait there for us."

"Yes, I will," Grandma said. I knew she meant it.

We left then for the drive back to Michigan, but returned a week later for Grandma's funeral. We would wear black that day. No other color would feel right on such a sad day.

I dressed and hurried to the kitchen where Aunt Mary had breakfast ready. Everyone was so kind to give us places to sleep with the number of relatives who had arrived for the funeral. Grandpa and Grandma had a large family of ten children and 41 grandchildren. The communities close by were also a great blessing by providing hot meals the past two days.

After breakfast the extended family gathered in Uncle Nelson's kitchen for devotions. Afterward we viewed Grandma's body again.

Four neighbor men carried the casket out to the large shop where benches had been set up the evening before.

I found my place in the second row with the other cousins. It was so special to see all the cousins, aunts, and uncles again, even though it was for Grandma's funeral. After everyone was seated, one of Grandma's favorite cousins, a minister, rose to his feet. He talked about salvation through Jesus Christ and the hope we have of meeting our departed loved ones again. He warned of the dangers if we neglect Christ's call and spoke comforting words of the reward for those who follow Christ. He finished and two more ministers preached. In closing, the bishop read Grandma's obituary and a poem I had written.

Tribute to Our Grandma

She was confident and cheerful,
She freely spoke her mind.
Accepted others as they were,
Her heart was big and kind.

Practical, industrious,
She dared to step ahead.
Standing strong at Grandpa's side,
They followed where God led.

She loved a bit of humor,
Some laughter and some fun.
Her children called her blessed,
As in Proverbs thirty-one.

Beauty shone through all her ways,
With caring words and deeds.
She's the first to leave our circle,
Let's follow where she leads.

After the bishop finished, one of the ushers opened the casket and a line of people came slowly from the back of the room to view the body one last time. I listened to the deacon read the comforting words of Psalm 91 as I watched people file past the casket. They were friends, nieces, nephews, cousins, and church members. Tears pricked my eyes. These were the people Grandma had labored with, the people she had loved. I hadn't cried much in the past few days. Grandma had been so sick and we had been glad she could be released from her suffering, but the ache in my heart still melted to tears as my shoulders shook with sobs. How we would miss Grandma! She had loved us so much. Beside me, two of my cousins, Esther Mae and Regina, were also crying. We pulled tissues from a box someone passed down the bench.

The usher now motioned for the grandchildren to go through the line. I wiped my eyes and paused beside the casket. I held Grandma's hand but I didn't linger long. This really wasn't Grandma. It was only an empty shell. In spite of the tears, deep in my heart was a calm joyfulness that Grandma was in a better place, though we would miss her. I cried some more as I took my seat and watched Grandpa and his children gather around the casket. Quiet sobbing filled the room. The family soon stepped back and the casket was gently closed.

Mom and Dad had borrowed a horse and buggy to drive to the cemetery, but we oldest children walked with the other cousins. The road was full of people heading to the cemetery. We hurried, walking between the buggies at times. At the cemetery Grandpa sat on his walker beside the freshly dug grave. Uncle Nelson stood beside him in support. The other aunts and uncles encircled the grave as we grandchildren gathered around them. Slowly the pallbearers lowered the casket into the rectangular hole. On top of the casket they placed a heavy rougher board.

Everyone watched quietly as the pallbearers began to shovel earth into the grave. From the back of the crowd a man's clear voice began to quote a German song.

"Gute Nacht, ihr meinen Lieben…" *Goodnight to you, my love.* He quoted the verse and several men sang the song in the slow tune we were all familiar with.

All forenoon the sky had been dreary gray, but now the clouds broke. The sun shone gently down on the group gathered in the cemetery. A soft breeze blew, carrying with it the sad yet lovely words of the song. A feeling of peace swept over me. This was so holy. It was so right. Grandma had toiled on the earth for 77 years; now her time to leave had come. She no longer needed this sick body, so we were gently returning it to the earth. The shovels clinked as they scooped up dirt and filled the grave.

Someone pushed a songbook into my hands. All of us grandchildren grouped together and someone began to sing "Precious Memories."

I took a deep breath and joined in. Grandma had liked to hear us sing this song for her. When the song soon ended, the pallbearers patted the mound of dirt smooth with their shovels. People started to leave, but first some of the grandchildren gathered small stones from the grave. They would take them home as a remembrance of Grandma. I hesitated. Did I really want a stone from Grandma's grave? Abruptly I made up my mind. I didn't care if the others gathered stones, but I wouldn't. I had other things to remember Grandma by. There was the quilt she had made, the scarf she had crocheted, and the painted sugar and creamer set she had given me.

Besides these things, I had the memories of Grandma when she was alive and able to bake cookies and bread, cook scrumptious meals, enjoy a good laugh, write newsy letters, and always welcome us into her home and heart. Indeed, I had many precious memories of Grandma from the past, and now I looked forward to meeting her again in the future.

Jerry Eicher taught for two terms in Amish and Mennonite schools in Ohio and Illinois. He writes of his experience growing up Amish in his memoir, *My Amish Childhood*. Jerry has been involved in church renewal, preaching, and teaching Bible studies. He lives with his wife, Tina, and their four children in Virginia.

Nathan Miller is an Amish family man and business owner. He's the author of one previous book, *Out of Deception*. Nathan makes his home in Michigan.

To learn more about Harvest House books and
to read sample chapters, visit our website:

www.harvesthousepublishers.com

HARVEST HOUSE PUBLISHERS
EUGENE, OREGON